66 Simple Rules for Entrepreneurs

Dean A. Shepherd · Holger Patzelt ·
Nicola Breugst

66 Simple Rules for Entrepreneurs

A Roadmap for Improved Performance

palgrave
macmillan

Dean A. Shepherd
University of Notre Dame
Notre Dame, IN, USA

Holger Patzelt
Technical University of Munich
Munich, Germany

Nicola Breugst
Technical University of Munich
Munich, Germany

ISBN 978-3-031-62031-7 ISBN 978-3-031-62032-4 (eBook)
https://doi.org/10.1007/978-3-031-62032-4

This work was supported by Technical University of Munich, TUM School of Management.

This Palgrave Macmillan imprint is published by the registered company Springer Nature Switzerland AG
The registered company address is: Gewerbestrasse 11, 6330 Cham, Switzerland

Acknowledgments

Justin Parer was the genesis of this book. Justin is a successful entrepreneur and one of Dean's best mates. He asked Dean for a few simple rules for entrepreneurial success. His request inspired this book.

We thank Ali Ferguson for her help with the manuscript and Bailen Murphy for creating the book cover.

Contents

1

Introduction

This book offers 66 simple rules for entrepreneurs. It is not a strictly academic book because it does not present specific research findings. We can assure you that the research underlying these rules is established and valid. If you are interested in the science behind the sections, we have compiled a list of further readings at the end of the book.

This book also differs from a textbook because we do not use detailed examples. While examples can help make abstract concepts more concrete, we go straight for the concrete. Hopefully, you can apply the simple rules to your specific context and do not need us to provide that context.

Of course, there are nuances to every one of these rules. However, if we delve into the nuances, they become more complex. One of the great entrepreneurship scholars, Kathie Eisenhardt, noted that for entrepreneurs the more complex and dynamic the environment, the simpler the rules need to be.[1] We have followed her recommendation

[1] Eisenhardt, K. M., & Sull, D. N. (2001). Strategy as simple rules. *Harvard Business Review, 79*(1), 106–176.

D. A. Shepherd et al., *66 Simple Rules for Entrepreneurs*,
https://doi.org/10.1007/978-3-031-62032-4_1

and offer simple rules. Some of these simple rules may apply to you, but others may not. While the book offers many simple rules, many others are not mentioned. We chose the simple rules that we thought were the most important rules for entrepreneurs.

The purpose of this book of simple rules is not to explain the process of entrepreneurship or why some groups of entrepreneurs perform better than other groups of entrepreneurs. Instead, this book is designed to give you tools we hope you can use to improve your entrepreneurial performance. We have structured these rules following the entrepreneurial journey. You will find rules for recognizing opportunities, selecting markets for entry, making decisions, and developing plans and strategies. We have included rules for collaborating with important others, such as engaging with external stakeholders, working with cofounders, and managing employees. You will also find tools to grow your venture, ride the emotional rollercoaster of the entrepreneurial journey, and develop the social aspects of your venture. Finally, the book also includes rules for managing mistakes and failures and exiting your venture.

We situate these simple rules in the entrepreneurial context. The entrepreneurial context is one of great complexity, dynamism, uncertainty, emotionality, time pressure, consequential outcomes, etc. It is a context in which decision-making cannot be formulated based on traditional decision analysis. There is no right approach to generate the right solution. In this context, your decision-making can substantially impact the quality of your decisions and thus your venture's performance.

We hope these simple rules help you consider your environment, venture, entrepreneurial team, and yourself. Good luck.

2

Simple Rules for Recognizing Opportunities

1 Simple Rule: When Others Constrain Your Career, Look for an Entrepreneurial Opportunity

Pursue an entrepreneurial career to overcome your employment constraints.

Many things may constrain us. In employment, bosses may tell you what to do, underappreciate your contributions, and believe that your work offers you few opportunities to develop your competencies. In an

These research articles provided important information in formulating the following simple rules for recognizing opportunities: (1) Amabile, T. M. (1997). Motivating creativity in organizations: On doing what you love and loving what you do. *California Management Review, 40*(1), 39–58. (2) Brown, T. (2008). Design thinking. *Harvard Business Review, 86*(6), 84–92. (3) Dyer, J. H., Gregersen, H. B., & Christensen, C. M. (2009). The innovator's DNA. *Harvard Business Review, 87*(12), 60–67. (4) Gaglio, C. M., & Katz, J. A. (2001). The psychological basis of opportunity identification: Entrepreneurial alertness. *Small Business Economics, 16*(2), 95–111. (5) Soyer, E., & Hogarth, R. M. (2015). Fooled by experience. *Harvard Business Review, 93*(5), 72–77. (6) Wiklund, J., Patzelt, H., & Dimov, D. (2016). Entrepreneurship and psychological disorders: How ADHD can be productively harnessed. *Journal of Business Venturing Insights, 6*, 14–20.

D. A. Shepherd et al., *66 Simple Rules for Entrepreneurs*,
https://doi.org/10.1007/978-3-031-62032-4_2

entrepreneurial career, you are the boss. Think about an entrepreneurial career as a chance to explore greater meaning in your work and life.

Use the freedom of entrepreneurship to craft your work and career.
Crafting is simply changing a task to suit your abilities and desires better—to fit you and your work better. Entrepreneurship provides the autonomy and independence to make substantial changes to the way you perform work. You can craft your entrepreneurial tasks to address your psychological needs, family concerns, and other factors to enhance the meaningfulness of your work and life. Consider what you want in your work and design your venture and role to provide these essentials.

Think about how your liabilities or disabilities can be assets.

What is a liability or a disability in employment? Can it represent an asset in the entrepreneurial context? If you face such limitations in your job, consider an entrepreneurial career.

2 Simple Rule: Invest Effort to Build Expertise from Your Experience

Recognize that experience is not necessarily expertise.
Experience is the number of years spent performing a task. Expertise is performing that task at a high or superior level. You hope your experience can lead to expertise, but that may not be true. For example, take a person who has spent many years making the same mistakes repeatedly. They are experienced but lack expertise. The issue arises when people believe they are experts simply because they have substantial experience. Recognize that your experience may not have led to expertise. You need to learn from your experience to develop expertise.

Use your failures to help build expertise.
The problem is that many people try to forget their failures and only learn from their successes; therefore, their experience does not build expertise. Learn from your failures to build expertise by conducting

postmortems. A postmortem involves deep reflection on a failure to understand its underlying causes. Another way to learn from failures is to focus on near misses. Near misses are often discounted as you may attribute the lack of negative consequences to luck. However, near misses are ideal learning opportunities because they are failures without the associated emotional baggage. They are an ideal opportunity for you to learn. By focusing on near misses and failures, you can challenge your intuition and improve it. For example, if using your intuition led to a near miss, this is an excellent opportunity to explore your intuition's consequences. It is a great learning opportunity.

Sometimes disagree with the group.

People often risk falling into groupthink, where they try to agree with other group members to be harmonious. While a harmonious group may feel good, task conflict enhances decision-making quality. Therefore, it is sometimes good to go against the group, to go against the grain, to disconfirm. Disagreeing with the group may generate experiences that build expertise.

Look for disconfirming evidence.

Like most people, you probably look for information that confirms your opinions and discount or ignore information that disconfirms your opinions. It's better to be more like a scientist who forms hypotheses and looks for disconfirming evidence to puncture holes in hypotheses. It would be best to disconfirm a hypothesis early rather than have it disconfirmed by others later when the costs are far greater. If you have worked hard to disconfirm your hypothesis and cannot do so, then you can have confidence in it and act on it.

Lose your focus.

You may value your ability to focus on issues. Focusing narrows your perspective to what is essential and helps you deal with expected issues, problems, opportunities, and threats. However, sometimes, it is good to lose focus and see the big picture. The big picture can highlight areas that you have failed to search. This notion of losing focus is consistent with the old saying, "Not losing the forest for the trees." We are not suggesting that you always rely on the big picture. Instead, we suggest that it can be beneficial to oscillate between focusing and losing focus—that is, switching between detailed and concrete issues (i.e., the trees) and big-picture abstract issues (i.e., the forest).

3 Simple Rule: Don't Be Fooled by Your Experience

Don't necessarily rely on your experience as a guide because your filters may lead you astray.

You may think that your experience provides you with expertise. Our surroundings are filtered before they enter our minds. We are bounded rationally, so we have limited attention and cognitive resources. We manage our limited capabilities by being cognitive misers—we like to create and use mental shortcuts.

Avoid focusing only what you can see.

You might think that you see everything happening, but you (like all people) often miss things right before you. You have cognitive blind spots. If you do not acknowledge your potential blind spots, you will be overconfident in your decision-making and surprised when the unexpected happens.

Don't attribute outcomes to protect your ego.

Like everyone, you tend to attribute successes to your skills and abilities and failures to external causes. This fundamental attribution error is functional in protecting your ego. It is dysfunctional in providing you with information critical for learning. Also, you are more likely to remember your successes than your failures. Therefore, when searching your memory for information as an input to decision-making, you emphasize information based on successes but discount information based on failures. Therefore, your experience can lead to superstitious learning by overemphasizing successes and underemphasizing failures as sources of information.

Focus more on the process than the outcomes of your actions.

Focusing on the outcomes of your actions can lead you astray. In an uncertain environment, we cannot be assured that doing the right things leads to the best outcome. In the long run, if we have the right process, then, on average, we will achieve the best outcomes. Therefore, focusing on a single outcome and changing our actions based on it may lead to superstitious learning.

Avoid confirmation bias by seeking disconfirming evidence.

People often cherry-pick information to support their opinions, ideas, or perspectives. That is, they may search for information that confirms their approach and ignore or discount information that suggests they are wrong. Although this confirmation may provide some comfort in the short term, it provides a distorted picture of learning and can hurt performance in the long run. Act like a scientist and seek disconfirming information; your hypothesis is supported if you cannot find evidence that refutes it.

Avoid hindsight bias by realizing that entrepreneurial decision-making is often shrouded in uncertainty.

You probably know the sayings "Being a Monday morning quarterback" and "Hindsight is 20/20." These sayings mean that it may seem easy to make the correct decision after the fact while looking back at an event. However, entrepreneurial decisions and actions are less evident in the moment because they are shrouded in uncertainty.

4 Simple Rule: Use Entrepreneurship as a Channel to Express Yourself

Work on an opportunity that meets your personal preferences and values.

Entrepreneurship can be a channel to express your values and personality; your unique personal values and preferences can be the source of new business opportunities. Sit down and inventory what you value and enjoy in life. Make these things an integral part of what you develop as your business.

Build your venture in a way that fits your personality.

When you build your venture, define your tasks and roles to fit your personality. If you are outgoing, you may want to focus on attracting investors and other stakeholders. If you like numbers, you may see yourself as the person dealing with your venture's accounting and financials. If your passion is technology, you can decide to take over responsibility as your venture's chief technology developer. Try to find cofounders or employees who take on what you like less.

Focus on the potential upside of your disadvantages.

You may experience some disadvantages and think they represent challenges for your career. However, disadvantages can sometimes represent opportunities for developing your entrepreneurial career. Indeed, your disadvantage may be an advantage under certain conditions. For example, famous entrepreneurs like Ingvar Kamprad (IKEA), David Neeleman (Azul Airlines), and Richard Branson (Virgin) are believed to have ADHD, which facilitates quick decision-making in complex situations. Disadvantages may also make you aware of specific problems you can address with your opportunity. For example, Whitney Wolfe Herd (Bumble) turned her experience with online harassment into an alternative dating app to break traditional patterns in online dating. Thus, even disadvantages can become a part of your business opportunity.

Develop antennas for your environment.

Some people are said to have "antennas" for certain environmental developments. These people are alert to opportunities that emerge from environmental changes. You can develop antennas for what you believe to be important for your life by systematically observing developments around you and your venture that may turn into new business opportunities. If you believe these opportunities may be potentially more interesting later, shelve them (note them) and come back to them regularly for reevaluation.

5 Simple Rule: To Design Value, Look for Disruptions (in Users and Your Environment)

Be creative to address problems.

Creativity involves a novel and useful outcome. Novelty is offering something new. Usefulness helps people overcome existing problems or perform current tasks more effectively. Without creativity, it is unlikely that you will be able to offer potential customers sufficient value that they demand your product or service. Focusing on solving people's problems helps ensure that you generate novel outcomes that are useful to some.

Focus on humans for inspiration, ideation, and implementation.

One source of opportunities can be the problems individuals (which may include you) have when performing specific tasks or obtaining desired outcomes. These problems can be a source of inspiration for entrepreneurship. Still, entrepreneurs must also generate solutions to these problems and exploit the focal opportunity so people can purchase the product/service.

Tap into your emotions and cognitive tools to be creative.

Emotions can be an excellent source of information. Empathy means that you can understand and share someone's emotional and cognitive experiences. This enhanced understanding and sharing can help you better understand the problems people face and how these problems can be solved. You can also rely on your optimism because it provides a positive vision of the future and the belief that you can successfully solve current problems. Similarly, you can use the scientific method to be creative by forming and testing hypotheses to reveal new information, which you can use to formulate new hypotheses to be tested and to continue moving an innovative idea forward.

Engage others to generate new ideas.

You can engage others in brainstorming and other processes to generate and access diverse information from people from different backgrounds. You can also develop rudimentary prototypes to visually depict an opportunity to facilitate discussion. Discussion about a prototype can provide critical feedback to refine your current potential opportunity; it provides critical input for creativity. A prototype only needs to be sufficiently developed to generate discussion. If the prototype is highly developed, people will be reluctant to change it and learning is lost.

Look in the usual places for incremental opportunities but in unexpected places for radical opportunities.

Your knowledge and experience contribute to a mental map that guides your attention to where you expect changes. These changes are likely to reflect incremental opportunities. However, relying on your mental map will likely result in you missing signals of more radical opportunities that are not in your immediate funnel of focused attention. To identify radical opportunities, you need to lose focus to broaden your attention to capture unexpected environmental changes. Losing focus (i.e., disengaging your mental map) allows your attention to be drawn to prominent environmental changes. By oscillating between focusing and losing focus, you can attempt to identify both incremental and radical opportunities. However, losing focus can be a challenging task.

6 Simple Rule: Motivate Creativity to Generate Opportunities

Be creative to generate opportunities.

As an entrepreneur, you need to be creative. You need to be creative to come up with potential opportunities, combine resources to alleviate resource constraints, and tell stories to access resources. You must also be creative in many ways, such as generating novel and useful outcomes. In addition, for your venture to be creative, you must encourage venture members to be creative.

Appreciate different forms of creativity.

Creativity can come in different forms. On the one hand, you can be creative by following some rules and thinking about idea refinements. This approach is a convergent form of creativity. For example, you can think about how some ideas might be applied to different domains, such as taking ideas from one market and introducing them to another. On the other hand, creativity can be divergent and involve some revolutionary ideas that are new to the world and break out of established thinking patterns. While you can trigger convergent creativity by engaging in structured processes of comparing and extending ideas, divergent creativity is less manageable. However, convergent creativity can help you evaluate and refine ideas arising from divergent creativity.

Engage intrinsic motivation to facilitate creativity.

Creativity requires effort. Motivate yourself and others to invest the necessary effort to be creative. Intrinsic motivation enhances creativity. Intrinsic motivation reflects an interest in the process of inquiry—the journey. Extrinsic motivation reflects the desire for rewards from others, focuses mainly on outcomes, and can diminish intrinsic motivation focused on the process. It is tough to enhance creativity by focusing on outcomes; you must focus on the process.

Engage prosocial motivation to facilitate creativity.

Prosocial motivation is the willingness to invest effort and other resources with the primary goal of benefiting others. Helping other people can provide the energy necessary to fuel the creativity process. Focus on people's problems to stimulate your prosocial motivation for creativity.

7 Simple Rule: Adopt an Entrepreneurial Mindset to Learn and Generate New Things

Engage your entrepreneurial mindset to identify and evaluate potential opportunities.

Potential opportunities come in many forms: you can recognize an opportunity for which products or services are not yet offered, develop a new market and/or technology for opportunity creation, or work with potential stakeholders to co-construct an opportunity. You can engage your entrepreneurial mindset to identify a potential opportunity by performing the following activities.

Engage your entrepreneurial mindset by associating things.

Associating is about connecting things. These things can be from different sources and may not normally be connected but may produce something novel and hopefully useful when combined. You can associate through bricolage by noticing the resources you have at hand and combining them for a purpose not originally conceived. You can associate by bringing together divergent thoughts, perspectives, and/or resources and combining them to "connect the dots" for an innovative solution.

Engage your entrepreneurial mindset by questioning things.

For example, you can ask "why" three times to begin understanding the root causes of a problem. Another question might be, what is on the flipside? That is, if everyone is looking at a phenomenon from one perspective, you may reveal new insights by taking an opposing or different perspective on the same phenomenon. With an entrepreneurial mindset, you will likely question existing constraints and whether they unnecessarily limit current thinking and action.

Engage your entrepreneurial mindset by observing others.

You may gain insights into product or service problems by watching others. For example, people may have created workarounds to solve their problems but may not even realize they have done so. Observation provides the sort of information people are unwilling or unable to communicate. The ultimate form of observation is to immerse yourself in an individual's context to gain insights into their experiences, especially their frustrations.

Engage your entrepreneurial mindset by experimenting.

You can experiment by forming a hypothesis (e.g., a conjecture about one of the assumptions underlying an opportunity), testing that hypothesis, and using information from the test to support the hypothesis (when the test reveals confirming evidence) or reject the hypothesis (when the test reveals disconfirming evidence). You can use that information to formulate a new hypothesis if the original hypothesis is rejected. You may want to test the most critical assumptions underlying an opportunity first (better to know fatal flaws earlier than later) or test the cheapest assumption first (learn at a low cost).

Engage your entrepreneurial mindset by networking.

Networking can provide access to resources. Indeed, networking (through acquaintances) can provide diverse chunks of information critical for generating novel and useful solutions. You can also use your network of family and friends (i.e., strong ties) when trust is critical to your entrepreneurial activity. Networking may also involve you reconnecting with dormant ties, associating with a high-status person or business, and connecting with a broker (i.e., a person or venture that can connect you to new people or groups).

3

Simple Rules for Market Selection and Entry

1 Simple Rule: Identify a Broad Opportunity Set from Which to Choose the "Best" One

Look in expected places to notice incremental changes and opportunities.

It seems obvious to advise you to look for opportunities where you expect to see them, but realize that these opportunities will likely be incremental. They can offer minor adjustments to your current offerings. They are incremental because your knowledge and experience direct you

These research articles provided important information in formulating the following simple rules for market selection and entry: (1) Choi, Y., & Shepherd, D. (2004). Entrepreneurs' decisions to exploit opportunities. *Journal of Management, 30*(3), 377–395. (2) Gruber, M., MacMillan, I. C., & Thompson, J. D. (2008). Look before you leap: Market opportunity identification in emerging technology firms. *Management Science, 54*(9), 1652–1665. (3) Kirtley, J., & O'Mahony, S. (2023). What is a pivot? Explaining when and how entrepreneurial firms decide to make strategic change and pivot. *Strategic Management Journal, 44*(1), 197–230. (4) Klaukien, A., Shepherd, D. A., & Patzelt, H. (2013). Passion for work, non-work related excitement, and innovation managers' decision to exploit new

D. A. Shepherd et al., *66 Simple Rules for Entrepreneurs*,
https://doi.org/10.1007/978-3-031-62032-4_3

to domains consistent with the past. Therefore, they offer a continuation of your current product/service/technology trajectory.

Switch to bottom-up attention allocation to identify discontinuous changes and opportunities.
To identify opportunities in unexpected places, you may need to disengage your experience and knowledge to allow environmental signals to capture your attention. These signals may indicate opportunities that are unexpected and perhaps more radical or disruptive to your current trajectory. This reliance on environmental stimuli to capture your attention represents a bottom-up process of allocating attention.

When using a bottom-up approach, be aware that you may focus on the irrelevant.

With a bottom-up approach, your attention is drawn to prominent environmental stimuli. Prominent does not necessarily mean relevant or profitable. Therefore, you must be careful that a bottom-up process does not distract you with prominent but irrelevant environmental signals.

Use guided bottom-up processes of attention.
Rather than focus solely on top-down or bottom-up attention-allocation processes, you can oscillate between the two. That way, you can identify potentially radical opportunities consistent with your knowledge, allowing for rapid evaluation and the capabilities necessary for exploitation.

product opportunities. *Journal of Product Innovation Management, 30*(3), 574–588. (5) Seyb, S. K., Shepherd, D. A., & Williams, T. A. (2019). Exoskeletons, entrepreneurs, and communities: A model of co-constructing a potential opportunity. *Journal of Business Venturing, 34*(6). (6) Shepherd, D. A., & Gruber, M. (2021). The lean startup framework: Closing the academic–practitioner divide. *Entrepreneurship Theory and Practice, 45*(5), 967–998. (7) Shepherd, D. A., McMullen, J. S., & Ocasio, W. (2017). Is that an opportunity? An attention model of top managers' opportunity beliefs for strategic action. *Strategic Management Journal, 38*(3), 626–644. (8) Shepherd, D., Sattari, R., & Patzelt, H. (2022). A social model of opportunity development: Building and engaging communities of inquiry. *Journal of Business Venturing, 37*, 106,033.

2 Simple Rule: Think Like a Scientist to Generate Novel Business Models or Opportunities

Form hypotheses to validate assumptions (critical or cheap).
Whether from your knowledge and experience, a hunch, or environmental signals, the scientific approach involves forming and testing a hypothesis. A hypothesis reflects an assumption that underlies an opportunity. It is probably best to test the most critical assumption first. The most critical assumption is the one an opportunity hinges upon—that is, if this assumption is found to be false, the viability of the whole potential opportunity is undermined. While you may want your hypothesis to be supported, it's better to know that an opportunity has a fatal flaw early in the process rather than later. Later, more time and money will be invested in the opportunity. At best, this means that opportunity termination is more expensive than it needs to be. At worst, these sunk costs may encourage you to persist with this losing course of action. An alternative to hypothesizing and testing the most critical assumption first is perhaps formulating and testing the cheapest assumption. If the testing cheapest assumption disconfirms the hypothesis, then you have been able to learn (to terminate the opportunity) at the lowest cost.

Design tests to disconfirm hypotheses.
It is somewhat natural to fall in love with your idea, seek information that supports it, and ignore or discount information that does not. However, such a process can lead you astray, causing you to persist with an opportunity that lacks sufficient promise. A scientist does the opposite. They test their hypotheses by searching for information to disconfirm their hypotheses. You need to seek information that would invalidate the hypothesized assumption underlying the focal opportunity. Only after searching for disconfirming evidence and not finding any can you claim that this hypothesis is supported. Then, it would be best if you moved on to formulate and test the next hypothesis.

Embrace your doubts to drive inquiry.

People often overlook the limitations of their thinking. This ignorance can lead you to commit to a course of action that generates feedback indicating that you should not have pursued this course of action in the first place. Rather than ignore limitations, you can embrace them as doubt. While doubt obstructs action, it can also fuel inquiry, such as forming and testing hypotheses. Testing hypotheses can reduce doubt and thus reduce the obstacles to entrepreneurial action. However, testing hypotheses may confirm doubts, giving you greater confidence in changing from your current approach (e.g., the current potential opportunity, business model, and/or strategy).

Be aware of errors with hypothesis findings.

Even the scientific approach to the entrepreneurial process can lead to errors (not surprising given the high uncertainty). A test can lead to a Type 1 error. A Type 1 error is a false positive, which means that you conclude from the evidence that your hypothesis is supported (e.g., the signals represent an attractive opportunity) when, in reality, the hypothesis should have been rejected. A test can also lead to a Type 2 error. A Type 2 error is a false negative, which means you reject your hypothesis because the evidence suggests it is false, but that conclusion is wrong (i.e., the hypothesis is right). Of course, it is hard to know whether you have an error. However, it is useful to remember that tests can reveal information that leads you to the wrong conclusion. It may be useful to sometimes reevaluate and retest a hypothesis or a related hypothesis.

3 Simple Rule: With Resource Constraints, Embrace the Lean Startup Approach

Construct a business model.
A business model explains how a venture (newly created or established) will exploit an opportunity and make money from it. Multiple experiments generate information about the business model. These multiple experiments might reveal that the business model needs to be refined or changed somehow (also see the second-to-last point on pivoting or terminating).

Engage in validated learning.
Validated learning involves seeking and analyzing the assumptions underlying an opportunity (or business model) and finding evidence supporting or rejecting these assumptions. You can generate information for validated learning by forming and testing hypotheses about the fundamental assumptions underlying a potential opportunity and searching for evidence that disconfirms these hypotheses. Information can come from experiments in your mind in which such hypotheses are formulated and tested to reveal information for learning.

Build minimum viable products.

A minimum viable product is a version of a product that is rudimentary but sufficient to communicate the product concept to others (e.g., potential stakeholders). By communicating the product concept, the minimum viable product can stimulate discussion and feedback, enabling you to learn and improve the ideas behind the product. It may lead to a new and improved minimum viable product.

Overcome psychological constraints to pivot or terminate an underperforming opportunity.
A pivot is a substantial change in direction from your previous approach. Termination is when a potential opportunity is killed because signals indicate poor performance; resources can then be redeployed to potential opportunities that show greater promise. You will likely find it difficult

to pivot or terminate your original idea (because you have a personal commitment to it). Think about your original idea as a basis to learn, so if you pivot or terminate it, it still creates value as a critical source of learning for moving forward.

Develop a portfolio of opportunities.
A portfolio of opportunities allows you to experiment with different opportunities that act like probes in an uncertain environment. They reveal information that could not otherwise be gained. Use this information to terminate potential opportunities that do not show promise, and redeploy resources to those that do show promise. Experimenting and probing in this way give you the right to pursue a potential opportunity but not the obligation; you can terminate it with little cost. Ensure the opportunities in your portfolio are not similar or highly related because multiple experiments in the same space provide overlapping information and do not "reveal" as much information about the environment as more diverse experiments.

4 Simple Rule: Create, Use, and Adapt a Community of Inquiry to Evaluate and Co-construct an Opportunity

Don't wait for the solo aha moment.

Creation can come in different forms and may involve others in the opportunity-development process. You may want to engage others in brainstorming, ideation, and idea refinement. The diversity others bring can provide critical perspectives for generating creative outcomes. Rather than waiting for a brilliant idea to strike you, interact with others in the ways detailed below.

Create and use a community of inquiry to co-construct an opportunity.
A community of inquiry is a collection of groups that could be (or are) your stakeholders. A community of inquiry can provide information and

support for a potential opportunity as it is developed and refined. You can select a community of inquiry around your potential opportunity to help construct it—that is, to build and refine the potential opportunity. This community of inquiry that co-constructs a potential opportunity may also be critical in exploiting the opportunity. Choose members of your community of inquiry who can help construct your opportunity, will benefit from a refined opportunity, and can facilitate opportunity exploitation.

Develop a two-way flow of information.
Entrepreneurs are told to continually pitch their ventures. However, sometimes, you should pause after a pitch and listen. Actively listening to feedback—even negative feedback—from your community of inquiry can reveal necessary information and strengthen potential stakeholders' commitment to your emerging opportunity and venture.

Focus on social learning and refining opportunities.
Rather than relying on your past experiences and knowledge, you can tap into others' knowledge to enhance the venturing process. To maximize social learning, be open to others' input (early and often), including negative feedback. Indeed, you can learn the most from social interactions that reveal information that disconfirms hypotheses about the validity of a potential opportunity's underlying assumptions. Use this information to make further adjustments to your opportunity (including a pivot or termination). You may find that pivoting in a new direction or terminating the opportunity requires you to go against your natural inclinations to persist.

Be prepared to change the composition of your community of inquiry.
As an opportunity is refined or otherwise changed, the community of inquiry surrounding it may also need to be changed given the nature of the new opportunity and the community needed to advance it. For example, as an opportunity takes a concrete form (from co-construction), the experts and others engaged in the ideation process become less important, and it becomes more critical to add potential suppliers and

distributors to the community of inquiry. Match the composition of your community of inquiry to the stage of the opportunity-development process you are in.

5 Simple Rule: If Your Opportunity Does Not Work Out, Pivot

Be prepared to change the direction of your venture.

A pivot is a substantial change in direction from a previous approach. While such changes can demand substantial resources from you and your venture, they are often necessary to find the best market for a technology or product. Making these changes is nothing extraordinary; indeed, most ventures pivot at different stages of their development (more often early than late). Don't be afraid of these changes; they often lead to a better outcome for you and your venture.

Build on your experience to do better.

If you decide to pivot, one key question is where to go next. Your experience can help you find the right new market or technology. Your prior experience provides knowledge about markets, customers, and technologies that may point you in a new direction and help you identify a new opportunity. Perhaps even more importantly, based on your experience, you can also identify experts who can help you validate ideas for new markets and technologies, and you can use your networks to acquire first customers for your venture's new offerings. If you have pivoted before, all the better—this type of experience can help you gain support from your cofounders and employees and thus gain momentum for your venture's new trajectory.

Overcome psychological constraints to pivot or terminate an underperforming opportunity.

Sometimes, we are locked into a course of action even if our environment signals a need for change. You will likely find it difficult to pivot or terminate your original idea (because you have a personal commitment to it). Think about your original idea as a basis to learn, so if you pivot or terminate it, it still creates value for you as a critical source of learning for moving forward.

Consider different types of pivots.
Not all pivots are alike, and executing a pivot can be a lengthy process at times. When searching for opportunities to pivot, you might consider adding new elements (products, technologies) to your business. However, you may also (perhaps in addition) decide to terminate some of your venture's prior activities, focusing on the remaining elements instead. Decide which way to proceed based on the information you acquire from experts and potential (and perhaps existing) customers. Both ways can take your venture in a new direction, making it better prepared for the challenges in the marketplace.

4

Simple Rules for Entrepreneurial Decision-Making

1 Simple Rule: Entry Decisions Are Complex, so Time Them Right

Choose the right time for entry.

The timing of market entry is important for all entrepreneurs. If you enter early, you may enjoy a first-mover advantage that helps you learn ahead of competitors and secure access to important customers or

These research articles provided important information in formulating the following simple rules for entrepreneurial decision-making: (1) Eisenhardt, K. M. (1990). Speed and strategic choice: How managers accelerate decision making. *California Management Review, 32*(3), 39 – 54. (2) Kanze, D., Huang, L., Conley, M. A., & Higgins, E. T. (2018). We ask men to win and women not to lose: Closing the gender gap in startup funding. *Academy of Management Journal, 61*(2), 586 – 614. (3) Keeney, R. L., & Raiffa, H. (2006). The hidden traps in decision making. *Harvard Business Review, 84*(1), 118. (4) Pohlmann, T., & Thomas, N. (2015). *Relearning the Art of Asking Questions*. Harvard Business Review,. (5) Sarasvathy, S. D. (2001). Causation and effectuation: Toward a theoretical shift from economic inevitability to entrepreneurial contingency. *Academy of Management Review, 26*(2), 243 – 263. (6) Shepherd, D. A., Parida, V., & Wincent, J. (2020). The surprising duality of jugaad: Low firm growth and high inclusive growth. *Journal of Management Studies, 57*(1), 87 – 128. (7) Soll, J. B., Milkman, K. L., & Payne, J. W. (2015). Outsmart your own biases. *Harvard Business Review, 93*(5), 64 – 71.

D. A. Shepherd et al., *66 Simple Rules for Entrepreneurs*,
https://doi.org/10.1007/978-3-031-62032-4_4

suppliers. On the downside, however, you may be prone to make many mistakes because you can't learn from the experience of others already in the market. If you enter late, learning from others in the market can help reduce your development costs and risks. However, those ahead may make securing critical resources and customer access difficult. Consider these pros and cons of being first when timing your entry.

Assess your resources when considering entry.

Entrepreneurs tend to enter the market earlier when they possess specific resources. When considering entry, evaluate the value potential customers will see in your product, how well your technology works, and how much others support your business. If these resources are developed well, you are closer to entering the market. In particular, these resources support entry when you have a considerable lead time compared to your competitors.

Build a strong team for entry.

Once you have decided that the time is ripe to enter the market, your venture needs to perform several different and complex activities, including ramping up production, establishing and maintaining customer relationships, and building distribution channels. To address all these issues, ensure you have a strong and large enough team with the necessary capabilities. You won't be able to oversee all these tasks yourself.

Be aware that your passion can trigger (too) early entry.

Entrepreneurs experiencing harmonious passion feel joy and energy when working on their ventures. When your passionate efforts lead to the possibility of entry coming up on the horizon, you may be tempted to enter as soon as possible. While early entry can be an advantage, make sure that your passion does not prevent you from allocating enough time to develop the resources needed for entry.

Consider that your life outside your venture may impact your entry decision.

Although, as a passionate entrepreneur, you may spend much of your time working on your venture, experiences outside of your venture can still impact how you make your entry decision. Positive life experiences can create positive emotions. If you are highly excited about such experiences, this excitement can further enhance the danger that your passion will speed up entry—perhaps too much. Be aware that this danger is extreme when your passion is obsessive—that is, when you feel you must work on your venture to be socially accepted and/or to have self-worth. Make sure you control your emotions from venture-external experiences when making your entry decision.

2 Simple Rule: If You Think You Do Not Have Implicit Biases, You Are Probably Wrong (We All Do), so Set Up Procedures to Circumvent Them

Be open to the idea that you have implicit biases.

In one study of men and women venture capitalists, these investors (regardless of their gender) asked women entrepreneurs questions about avoiding losses and men entrepreneurs questions about growing their businesses.[1] Unsurprisingly, men entrepreneurs were more likely to receive funding than women entrepreneurs despite the same venture quality. The venture capitalists were unaware of how gender drove their questions. It makes you think we may also be unaware of our implicit biases. Assume that it is at least possible that you have implicit biases and do something about them.

Develop and use systematic procedures to overcome implicit biases.

You can overcome implicit biases in several ways. You can ask the same questions to applicants (i.e., employees, suppliers, or potential investees). Work out what questions you will ask, and then you can engage the interviewees in the same "fair" way. You can also create checklists to make sure you consider each attribute of interest rather than forming a global impression of an individual. A global impression is likely to be more

[1] Kanze, D., Huang, L., Conley, M. A., & Higgins, E. T. (2018). We ask men to win and women not to lose: Closing the gender gap in startup funding. *Academy of Management Journal, 61*(2), 586–614.

influenced by implicit biases. Further, you can involve multiple respondents to highlight the appropriateness of your evaluations. However, remember the example of the venture capitalists above—multiple respondents can have the same implicit biases. The point is to try to make the process by which you make decisions more explicit, enabling you to be more deliberate in your decision-making and, therefore, less reliant on intuition. Implicit biases can have more of an impact when you make intuitive decisions. However, just because you use a more deliberate decision-making process does not mean that you are bias-free.

Allocate sufficient time to make crucial decisions.

By giving you and your team more time to decide, you can implement the above systematic procedures and put less pressure on relying on intuition to make a quick decision. The more you deliberate a decision, the more you can reduce implicit biases.

Use blind auditions to avoid implicit biases.

Think about how you can make your process blind to irrelevant features of performing the job task well. This could be, for example, taking the names and addresses off resumes to focus on people's achievements while remaining blind to their gender, ethnicity, and socioeconomic status.

Update your initial categories to reduce implicit biases.

People use stereotypes of individuals they meet for the first time to categorize them and make initial decisions about them. Such first impressions are natural. However, it is essential that as you gain more information, you invest the time and energy necessary to update your categorizations and evaluations of individuals. Categorizing people is not a problem, but failing to update these categories can be a problem.

3 Simple Rule: Reduce Your Overconfidence in Making Predictions

Make multiple estimates to reduce your overconfidence.

Rather than making one estimate, make two and take the average of the two. This approach can improve the accuracy of your estimates and open your mind to more than one possibility.

Use premortems to reduce overconfidence.

Premortems are thinking about all the things that could go wrong in your future course of action. Thinking about the things that could go wrong helps reduce your overconfidence and can prepare you to respond to these possibilities if they occur.

Take an outsider's perspective to reduce overconfidence.

Rather than considering your situation from your perspective of being fully embedded in it and your tasks, consider the perspective of an outsider—a detached but knowledgeable observer. What would an outsider think about your current situation, and how would they act? Such an approach helps provide a broader perspective, a more deliberate approach, and objectivity to the decision-making process.

Realize that more information is not always better.

Sometimes, more information merely confirms the information you already have. Indeed, this additional information may not improve your decision accuracy but can increase your confidence that you will make an accurate decision. In such a situation, you are particularly prone to increased overconfidence.

4 Simple Rule: While Slack is Nice, Necessity Can Be the Mother of Innovation

Use adversity to combine and use your resources for a different purpose.

Change your mindset from relying on slack resources for experimentation to a mindset of necessity. By thinking about necessity and resource constraints, you can engage in bricolage. Bricolage refers to using the resources you have at hand and combining and recombining them in unique ways to offer an innovative solution to the current problem you are trying to solve. Think MacGyver. People from India use the word *jugaad*. It is a lot like bricolage but emphasizes the iterative nature of the problem-solving process, which entails substantial trial and error. Jugaad also reflects the attitude of an innovator. You take on an assertive defiance, believing you can achieve success while being unwilling to take on other people's constraints. You break the rules to pursue worthwhile goals.

Consider inclusion (broader stakeholders) when innovating and growing.

Entrepreneurs have moved beyond a primary focus on shareholders to think more broadly about stakeholders. The notion of inclusive growth or inclusive innovation takes this new focus one step further. Traditionally, you would think about your cost structure and the people you should target who can afford a price that will give your venture a sufficient profit. Instead, an inclusive approach involves considering who needs your products and services and what cost structure you need to implement to deliver value to all people, including the impoverished.

5 Simple Rule: When You Lack Information to Make Decisions, Turn to What You Have at Hand

Let your knowledge and resources guide your decisions.

When you enter a new market, gathering information to make crucial decisions can be challenging. Instead, turn inward. You can make decisions based on your knowledge and resources. Make an inventory of your resources and be creative to imagine different goals you can achieve with these resources. Then, pick the goal you like most. If you learn it is harder to reach than imagined, be flexible and switch to another goal. Ultimately, your venture may look different than you first imagined, but it may be stronger than you ever thought it could be.

Turn to others to enhance your available resources.

While everyone has more knowledge and resources than they typically are aware of, others can increase their resource bases. Indeed, your network is itself a valuable resource. By talking to others in your environment, you can validate your decisions and perhaps gain their support for and commitment to your venture, thus enhancing your available resource pool.

Consider your resources to limit your investments.

With little knowledge about your market and potential financial returns, making decisions based on your project's or venture's expectancy or net present value is hard. Instead of considering future revenues, turn to your resources to assess the maximum you are willing to lose when investing in your project or venture. Set this maximum regarding financials and the time and effort you will invest into a project or your venture. Pull the plug if you have invested this maximum amount of resources without the desired outcome.

Form partnerships.

As a small venture owner, you often have insufficient resources to beat your competitors to the punch. Therefore, consider allying with your enemies. You can share costs, equipment, and office space with other firms in your environment. You can also form distribution and marketing partnerships with large companies that have built these capabilities over the years. By forming partnerships, you can capitalize on resources, knowledge, and competencies you do not have in-house.

6 Simple Rule: If You Want to Capture Fleeting Opportunities, Then Speed up Your Decision-Making

Don't seek less information; seek more, but make it real-time information.

Although skimping information to speed decision-making is tempting, your decision quality will suffer. To speed up decision-making, you need to use real-time information. Real-time information is information about your venture's operations in the moment and about your venture's external environment in the moment. This real-time information is raw and frequently changing, so it can be difficult to interpret. Rely on your intuition to notice and interpret signals of opportunities (or threats) from this real-time information.

Use meetings to generate real-time information.

Although some meetings may be a waste of time, good meetings can help speed up decision-making. Good meetings involve venture members who discuss real-time issues and problems. These discussions provide venture members with a big picture of the venture's various operations at the current time. These meetings may also reveal how real-time information can be used to take entrepreneurial action.

Build multiple simultaneous alternatives to make choices.

While it might seem quicker to rate alternatives in order and then choose the one that is satisfactory and sufficient, this is not the best decision-making approach. It is better to generate multiple alternatives representing the range and scope of a particular decision and then rank those alternatives. This ranking is quicker than rating, generates greater confidence in the final decision, and identifies a Plan B.

Encourage task conflict to find the best solution.

In meetings discussing real-time information, it is essential to foster task conflict. Conflict over which tasks should be performed and how they should be performed generates information for and enables better decisions. You should give people a voice and actively listen to that voice, but as the decision-maker, you must ultimately make the decision. One scholar (Eisenhardt) calls this "consensus with qualification." Discuss options within your team and try to reach consensus, but meetings cannot go on forever; ultimately, you have to decide. Venture members are likely to accept this approach so long as you allow them to express their opinions and you listen to those opinions even if you ultimately do not go in the direction they suggest.

Use intuition, perhaps through a counselor.

When dealing with real-time information, intuition may be helpful. Intuition may help you notice anomalies or signals in the real-time information representing opportunities or threats. Your intuition must be based on expertise; otherwise, it could lead you astray. One way to enhance your intuition is to have a counselor who is experienced in your venture's domain—a trusted advisor.

7 Simple Rule: Decision Analysis Will Only Get You so Far; Tap into Your Inner Child to Ask Questions

Don't rely on traditional decision analysis when facing high uncertainty.

Decision analysis involves formulating a problem, listing the courses of action to address the problem, systematically assessing those various courses, and choosing the one with the greatest expected value. However, decision analysis is useless in an uncertain environment, such as identifying and pursuing a potential opportunity, because the courses of action are unknown. It is impossible to put probabilities on the different courses of action to calculate their expected value. While decision analysis is effective for making decisions under risk, it is ineffective in the entrepreneurial context of high uncertainty.

Don't be frightened to ask questions.
Children show no fear in asking questions. They are curious and learn a lot. Don't be afraid of asking questions because you think it shows others you don't know the answers. In an uncertain environment, no one knows all the answers. The way to learn is to act and ask questions, gain information, and move forward.

Ask why and why-not questions.
Like a child asking questions, when you ask why and why-not questions, you challenge the status quo and provide an opportunity to learn. Challenging the status quo can be helpful because sometimes people follow procedures without asking whether they can improve them. As an entrepreneur, you will want to challenge the status quo sometimes.

Ask clarifying questions to understand issues.
Clarifying questions help you understand the nature of a problem or issue. You might ask the following: What problem do we face here? How is this problem similar to other problems we have faced? How is this problem different from other problems we have faced? What do you want to achieve in addressing this problem? Your decision-making process is severely undermined without fully understanding your current situation and task.

Ask adjoining questions to explore related aspects.
Ask adjoining questions to explore the boundaries of a current issue. For example, how can this technology be used in a different market? What other products can we generate from this technology? Answering questions like these allows you to broaden your thinking and perhaps generate innovative responses.

Ask funneling questions to dive deeper.
Funneling questions enhance your understanding by helping you move from a more superficial level of a problem or issue to a deeper,

richer understanding of the problem or issue. For example, when you ask why three times ("Why? Why? Why?"), the answer to the final "Why?" is likely to provide a better understanding of the underlying root causes of the focal problem or issue.

Ask elevating questions to see the big picture.
When dealing with an issue or a problem, you may get stuck in the weeds by focusing on the concrete details. There are also benefits from taking a big-picture perspective. By asking elevating questions, you can gain a big picture highlighting how the different pieces come together or what pieces are missing in the overall picture.

Ask metacognitive questions to question assumptions.
You may make decisions automatically and thus not have access to the underlying assumptions of your decisions. Asking metacognitive questions forces you to think about how you think. Metacognitive questions include the following: What is the situation I am facing here? How is this situation similar to other situations I have faced? How is this situation different from situations I faced in the past? What different strategies or approaches can be used to address the issue at hand? After choosing and pursuing an approach, asking yourself, "How I am doing?" allows you to reflect on whether you are pursuing the right action. When you make your decision process more explicit (to yourself and/or others), it is easier to question the validity of the assumptions driving your decisions and make adjustments before committing to a course of action.

5

Simple Rules for Developing Plans and Strategies

1 Simple Rule: Reflect on Your Personal Goals When Setting an Entrepreneurial Strategy

Ensure your conception of your venture delivers outcomes that are desirable to you.

How you think about an entrepreneurial strategy differs from how you think about a corporate strategy. With a corporate strategy, managers are required to pursue goals that shareholders desire. A venture can represent a vehicle for you to achieve your personal goals. Therefore, you must understand what you want to achieve personally through creating and running your venture. These desires could be to make lots of money, have a lifestyle business, or help people in need.

These research articles provided important information in formulating the following simple rules for entrepreneurial decision-making: (1) Bhide, A. (1996). The questions every entrepreneur must answer. *Harvard Business Review, 74*(6), 120. (2) Bohn, R. (2000). Stop fighting fires. *Harvard Business Review, 78*, 82–92. (3) Brinckmann, J., Grichnik, D., & Kapsa, D. (2010). Should entrepreneurs plan or just storm the castle? A meta-analysis on contextual factors impacting the business planning–performance relationship in small firms.

D. A. Shepherd et al., *66 Simple Rules for Entrepreneurs*,
https://doi.org/10.1007/978-3-031-62032-4_5

Consider feasibility, but don't feel too constrained by it.

In addition to assessing the desirability of your entrepreneurial action, you need to assess its feasibility. Your perception of feasibility is based on your assessment of whether you have the skills, knowledge, and resources to exploit a potential opportunity successfully. However, entrepreneurs are often unconcerned about whether they have all the resources needed for successful exploitation because they believe that if they have identified an attractive opportunity, they can somehow access the resources required to exploit it. Therefore, don't feel overly constrained by your immediate possession of or access to resources to exploit an opportunity.

Ask yourself if you want to be rich or be the king/queen?

This question highlights the founder's dilemma—namely, that the more successful you are as an entrepreneur, the more likely you are to be replaced as the manager of your organization. The logic goes as follows: The more successful your venture, the faster it grows, and to fund that growth, you need to raise funds from others. Raising these funds requires diluting your ownership of the venture. As the venture grows, the other owners may push to replace you as the venture's leader because running a larger organization requires different skills than starting one. Therefore, it is essential to understand whether you want to be rich or be the king/queen because if you want to be the king/queen of your venture, then you will need to make decisions to maintain control, such as growing

---

Journal of Business Venturing, 25(1), 24–40. (4) Eisenhardt, K. M., & Sull, D. N. (2001). Strategy as simple rules. *Harvard Business Review, 79*(1), 106–119. (5) McGrath, R. G., & Keil, T. (2007). The value captor's process: getting the most out of your new business ventures. *Harvard Business Review, 85*(5), 128–36. (6) Patzelt, H., Behrens, J., Wolfe, M. T., & Shepherd, D. A. (2020). Perceived project transition support and employees' assessments of entrepreneurial project performance. *Journal of Business Venturing, 35*(1), 1–25. (7) Preller, R., Patzelt, H., & Breugst, N. (2020). Entrepreneurial visions in founding teams: Conceptualization, emergence, and effects on opportunity development. *Journal of Business Venturing, 35*(2), 105,914. (8) Tryba, A., Patzelt, H., & Breugst, N. (2023). Knowledge diversity and venture growth: The contingent effects of early planning and experimentation. *British Journal of Management, 34*(1), 343–362. (9) Wasserman, N. (2017). The throne vs. the kingdom: Founder control and value creation in startups. *Strategic Management Journal, 38*(2), 255–277. (10) Watkins, M. D., & Bazerman, M. H. (2003). Predictable surprises: The disasters you should have seen coming. *Harvard Business Review, 81*(3), 72–85.

your venture at a slower pace and not seeking equity funding (at least not so much that you can lose control).

Know your desires and decide to craft a venture that delivers on those desires.

You need to know your desires to inform your decisions about what type of venture to create, what funding to seek, and how to manage growth. For example, being replaced as a founder may cause little concern for those motivated by money because they are likely to receive considerable wealth based on the growth and success of their ventures. However, those motivated by controlling their ventures will feel likely frustrated and disappointed from being replaced.

Build and test your self-knowledge about what you desire from your venturing activities.

This self-knowledge can come from reflecting on your plan for your venture and whether it will produce results consistent with your desires. You can also develop this self-knowledge by engaging in thought experiments—think about different venture outcomes, how you are likely to react to those outcomes, and which outcomes you prefer over others. This information can help you realize your preferences and, therefore, what venture outcomes you desire the most. Gain this self-knowledge earlier because delayed course corrections can be costly or too late.

Frequently pause and ask yourself if your venture is heading in a direction that will deliver the outcomes you desire most.

If you do not know your desires for venturing or do not learn about them as you progress, others who can push or pull your venture in directions that match their goals will decide for you. When others make such decisions, you will likely learn your preferences. However, it may be too late to do anything by then.

2 Simple Rule: Think About Your Venture's Future and Your Future in It

Write a business plan.

On many occasions, you will be asked to present your business plan. Indeed, business planning can be beneficial for the performance of your firm. On the one hand, it can help you have written documentation, including specific steps, goals, and budgets. This documentation allows you to check if your venture is still on track. Moreover, such a plan is essential to communicate with your stakeholders and to reduce doubts they might have about your venture. On the other hand, the activities connected to business planning, such as engaging in market analysis or detailed forecasting, can enhance your firm's performance. All these activities facilitate your learning about your firm. Therefore, having a written business plan (outcome) and engaging in business planning (process) can benefit you.

Tap into your team members' knowledge.

Engaging in business planning can also be helpful because it helps you coordinate your venture. In particular, when you work in a team of cofounders, a business plan can represent a scaffold, bringing together the activities necessary to develop your venture. Your teammates may have different areas of expertise, views, and responsibilities. Based on a business plan, you can combine all these contributions to benefit most from your team members' unique insights. Thus, planning can support your teamwork and help integrate team members' diverse contributions to your venture.

Think about yourself in relation to your venture's future.

Many people will tell you to develop a vision for your venture. This vision will enable you to see your venture's ideal future development and capture its core values. Furthermore, this vision can inspire your employees and potential investors. Indeed, for a young venture, your vision projects your current venture into the future. Instead of developing a vision for your venture independent of a vision for your future, ask yourself how long you want to stay in your venture. Do you see yourself spending your entire career in this venture as (one of) the owner(s)? Are you considering starting a new venture after some years? Could you imagine being acquired by another company and working for them? The answers to these questions have different implications for how you develop your venture. For example, engaging institutional investors can make it more likely that you will need to exit your venture after some years. Thus, an entrepreneurial vision helps you to develop a notion of yourself and your venture in the future while providing you with clear ideas on how to develop (yourself and your venture) in the present.

3 Simple Rule: When Facing Uncertainty, Look for Ways to Capitalize on Learning (Stage Gates Won't Cut It)

Be wary of using the stage-gate process (go or no go).

Although the stage-gate process effectively reduces escalation of commitment to a losing project, it assumes that we can set the gates and the criteria for a "go" or "no go" from the beginning. However, for more novel opportunities, you will face greater uncertainty, so setting the stage gates at the beginning becomes difficult (if not impossible) and severely restricts your ability to learn and adapt your entrepreneurial course of action.

Experiment.

Rather than stage gates, think of experiments. Formulate a hypothesis and then seek information to disconfirm that hypothesis. Regardless of whether the hypothesis is supported, the test reveals information you can use to formulate your next step—perhaps your next hypothesis. The process continues and provides opportunities to learn and adapt based on that learning.

Create and manage a portfolio of opportunities.

Think of each opportunity as a probe into an uncertain environment. Each probe reveals information. Use that information to terminate potential opportunities that do not show promise and redeploy resources to those that do show promise. This portfolio approach is consistent with the trial and error of experiments for one potential opportunity but across many potential opportunities.

Be prepared to terminate early and often, but make sure you learn.

When you consider opportunities as the basis for experiments within a portfolio of opportunities, you have an entrepreneurial mindset toward terminating potential opportunities early. Terminating opportunities early as part of a portfolio approach means you have invested less in any one opportunity. Therefore, there are fewer sunk costs to encourage you to escalate your commitment. Even the potential opportunities that do not pan out provide important information. Learn from that information as you move your venture forward.

Capitalize on learning from opportunities that do not show promise.

Rather than terminating an opportunity and forgetting about it, consider whether you should keep many of the same resources accumulated and pivot to a new strategic direction. Can you transfer the progress made so far to another part of your organization that can benefit from it or even sell this progress to someone outside your organization? Even with a complete termination, it is worth considering whether you can salvage some of the value created—don't throw the baby out with the bath water.

Construct a team to review new ventures.

If you created and developed a particular opportunity, you may not be the right person to assess its progress and whether a change is needed. By creating a team to evaluate the opportunity, there is a greater chance that the decision will be unaffected by biases. You can create a team of people that includes outside experts, others within your venture not involved with the focal project but who could benefit from what has been learned, and/or those responsible for exploiting the potential opportunity at scale.

4 Simple Rule: Simplify Your Rules as the Environment Becomes More Complex and Dynamic

Formulate your entrepreneurial strategy as simple rules.

Simple rules are rules of thumb that guide the actions of venture members but also allow members to operate within these guidelines. In a complex and dynamic environment, simple rules provide some guidance. However, within those broad guardrails, they offer considerable freedom in responding to environmental changes. Strategizing using simple rules allows you to make quick decisions, act, and receive feedback from those actions. Quick decisions and actions in dynamic environments are critical to trial-and-error learning and moving forward.

Embrace the chaos of high-velocity environments.

You will likely face a high-velocity environment because that is where opportunities can be found or constructed. It is best to jump into the chaos to capture fleeting opportunities. You can implement simple rules that offer some guidance despite the incredible uncertainty. Therefore, jump into the chaos and shift flexibly based on your simple rules.

Develop your simple rules based on a few of your key strategic processes.

The simple rules you implement will likely come from your past experiences and reflect your capabilities. Simple rules can be categorized as follows: Generate picking rules to help you choose between alternatives quickly. Generate boundary rules to help you quickly decide whether something should or should not be pursued. Generate process rules to guide you in how tasks should be performed. Generate exit rules to guide your decisions on when and how to exit a project, opportunity, or task.

Formulate between five to seven rules.

People can remember up to seven chunks of information. If there are more than seven simple rules, the simplicity is lost because people may not remember each rule. Venture members must remember all the rules to ensure everyone is on the same page.

5 Simple Rule: Be Aware of and Minimize Your Venture's Vulnerabilities

Be aware that the information you receive may be heavily filtered.

Although most entrepreneurial ventures do not have a hierarchical structure, those that do may be particularly vulnerable to information being filtered on the way up to you as the boss. Each person at each level may be motivated to provide a rosy picture or ingratiate themselves with the person above them. If you are concerned about these resulting vulnerabilities, you may want to use a flatter organizational structure to reduce information filtering. However, a flatter organizational structure may make your whole organization move more slowly. Another way to avoid filtering information through layers of management is for you to empower lower-level employees to notice and respond to signals of threats.

Connect your venture's information silos.

A venture has different silos when groups work independently of each other within the venture. These silos can mean that information is not exchanged efficiently or effectively across the venture, negatively impacting its threat response. To overcome silos, you can create cross-functional teams that work together, share information, and perhaps take information back to their siloed groups. You could also engage information brokers. Brokers are people who connect different groups from different silos. These connections can facilitate the exchange of information. Furthermore, information can be shared through informal networks within your venture. You can create these informal networks that cross functions and departments, facilitating the exchange of information for effective threat responses.

When threatened centralize decision-making.

Your venture will respond more effectively to local problems if you decentralize decision-making and empower those closest to where a problem occurs. However, threats to your entire venture may require a more coordinated response and a centralized decision-making process. You may need to be able to switch from decentralized to centralized or centralized to decentralized depending on the localness of threat signals.

Create a venture climate that eliminates politics.

You will likely want to get rid of politics. One way to avoid politics interrupting the flow of information between venture members is to institute a climate of psychological safety. In such a climate, venture members are willing to voice their concerns, including information about possible threats. If politics operate through the formal organizational structure and thereby reinforce power imbalances, you may want to rely on your informal networks to understand your vulnerabilities. You can also rely on experts' intuition for detecting and responding to vulnerabilities regardless of where the experts are in the organizational structure.

6 Simple Rule: Anticipate and Avoid (or Prepare for) Potential Threats

Recognize signals of potential surprises.

This recognition requires you to be aware of your surroundings and particularly sensitive to signals of threats regardless of whether they are where you expect them to be or elsewhere. It may be challenging to notice signals of threats, but increasing your motivation and knowledge of these potential sources can increase your sensitivity to detecting and interpreting them.

Prioritize signals of potential surprises.

Noticing and interpreting signals of potential surprises is insufficient. It would be best to prioritize those signals so you can better understand what they may mean and formulate a response, starting with the most salient.

Mobilize resources for a response.

Noticing, interpreting, and prioritizing signals of potential threats are important, but they must lead to you taking some action in response. That action could be some form of preparation for the anticipated event such that its negative implications would be reduced if it does occur.

Anticipating and avoiding predictable surprises might be easier said than done.

It makes sense to recommend that you take notice of signals in your environment, prioritize those representing threats, and respond to those potential threats. However, in the face of considerable uncertainty, it can be challenging to determine whether a signal is real or just noise. Err on the side that a signal represents a threat (vis-à-vis noise) when the cost of missing the threat would be substantial.

7 Simple Rule: Meetings Can Help Make Effective Transitions from One Project to the Next

Create and manage debriefing sessions to enhance learning.

A debriefing session is a meeting that typically occurs at the end of a project. The purpose of this meeting is to discuss what went well, what went poorly, what the outcomes were, and what could be done differently in the future to generate a better outcome. A debriefing session also signals that a project is complete and it is time to move on to the next project. Debriefing sessions are critical for learning. Provide a pause between projects so that you can reflect, learn, and prepare to move on. Debriefing sessions are especially beneficial when something goes wrong.

They are often called postmortems because the goal is to learn what caused a project's failure or death.

Create and manage briefing sessions to enhance learning. A briefing session occurs before a project begins. In such meetings, people discuss what the project goals are, who is to do what, how things will be executed, and what the expected outcomes are. Briefing sessions are vital because they ensure all venture members are on the same page. These briefing sessions lay down the assumptions and criteria for assessing a project after execution.

Create and manage premortem sessions to enhance learning. Premortems are meetings in which you discuss everything that could go wrong with an upcoming project. By highlighting what could go wrong, you pay attention to signals of these disruptions and are thus better prepared to respond if they occur. Thinking about what could go wrong might also help reduce your overconfidence. As all entrepreneurs, you are probably overconfident in your projects. A premortem can help reduce this overconfidence.

Engage in rigorous debate.

Whether it is a debriefing, briefing, or premortem, these meetings will only work if there is rigorous debate. You must ensure that different viewpoints are revealed and debated to improve the task. This task conflict can help generate better decisions and facilitate learning.

8 Simple Rule: Avoid Firefighting Mode to Improve Long-Run Performance

Solve the most critical problems first based on your goals and strategy. Sometimes, we are drawn to fix problems that are highly prominent or salient rather than those that are the most important for us to achieve our objectives. For example, we know that in organizations, the squeaky wheel often receives the oil (i.e., the employee who complains the most receives management's attention). It is essential to recognize and prioritize problems based on their importance for achieving your goals and strategy. Then, you can address the most important ones first.

Address causes rather than quick-fix solutions.

Because you are busy, you may be tempted to develop a band-aid solution for a problem. This approach only addresses the symptoms of the problem, and the cause will soon rear its ugly head. You need to invest the extra time to address the underlying causes of problems rather than simply addressing the symptoms. This approach means you will likely take a hit in the short term (i.e., the symptoms persist for longer) but obtain a long-term gain (i.e., spend less time in firefighting mode). In contrast, continually addressing the symptoms of a problem compounds the problem, severely diminishing your effectiveness as an entrepreneur.

Train people to solve problems.

You have likely been trained in many things, and you have likely trained other people in different tasks and situations. This training needs to be extended to yourself and others to learn how to solve problems effectively. While you cannot predict in advance what those problems will be, you can train people to engage in the problem-solving process to address the underlying causes of the problems they face and to address little problems before they become big problems.

Engage in preventative actions.

Again, you may not be able to predict what problems arise, but some issues are likely to reoccur. Engage in preventative actions that enable you to avoid or minimize a likely problem. Preventive actions allow you to choose when to address an issue so that it does not escalate into a major problem rather than react to a problematic event. Choose the timing of your response to prevent issues escalating into major problems.

6

Simple Rules for Engaging External Stakeholders

1 Simple Rule: Build a Circle of Trusted Advisors and Listen to Them

Seek honest feedback from yourself and others to try to overcome biases.

You may be dishonest with yourself (i.e., protect your ego), and others may not be entirely forthcoming with the truth. Whether deceiving yourself or being deceived by others, your decision-making quality will

These research articles provided important information in formulating the following simple rules for engaging external stakeholders: (1) Amabile, T., Fisher, C. M., & Pillemer, J. (2014). IDEO's Culture of Helping. *Harvard Business Review, 92*(1), 54–61. (2) Brown, C. (2015). *Know your worth, and then ask for it*. TEDxColumbusWomen. (3) Fauchart, E., & Gruber, M. (2011). Darwinians, communitarians, and missionaries: The role of founder identity in entrepreneurship. *Academy of Management Journal, 54*(5), 935–957. (4) Garvin, D. A., & Roberto, M. A. (2001). What you don't know about making decisions. *Harvard Business Review, 79*(8), 108–119. (5) Malhotra, D. (2014). 15 Rules for negotiating a job offer. *Harvard Business Review, 92*(4), 117–120. (6) Shepherd, D., Sattari, R., & Patzelt, H. (2022). A social model of opportunity development: Building and engaging communities of inquiry. *Journal of Business Venturing, 37*, 106033. (7) Soyer, E., & Hogarth, R. M. (2015). Fooled by experience. *Harvard Business Review, 93*(5), 72–77. (8) Uzzi, B., & Dunlap, S. (2005). How to build your network. *Harvard Business Review, 83*(12), 53–60.

D. A. Shepherd et al., *66 Simple Rules for Entrepreneurs*,
https://doi.org/10.1007/978-3-031-62032-4_6

deteriorate. You need to seek honest feedback even if receiving that feedback can be uncomfortable (for you or the person giving it to you).

Recognize that others' incentives and biases ***may impact the information you receive.***

Some people may tell you what you want to hear to ingratiate themselves with you or to avoid conflict. However, such filtered information can negatively impact the quality of your decisions. Furthermore, the people giving you information may be biased and error-prone. Understanding the quality of the information you receive is essential in weighing that information when making your entrepreneurial decisions.

Form and use a trusted circle of advisors to help you overcome the status quo bias.

A trusted circle of advisors can provide the information and the confidence to change your entrepreneurial course of action. The trust of trusted advisers is essential because when seeking help, you make yourself vulnerable to them. Advice from trusted advisers is critical in entrepreneurship, especially when these advisers are experts in your particular domain. They can provide the intuition you need to enhance your confidence and take entrepreneurial action that can change the status quo.

Don't shoot the messenger.

It is best to receive honest feedback from people. You can use that valuable information to learn, make better decisions, and enhance entrepreneurial performance. If you attack or show displeasure to people who give you negative feedback, they will be more reluctant to do so, and you will lose this vital source of learning.

2 Simple Rule: Don't Journey Alone; Involve Others Because Entrepreneurship Needs to Be a Social Endeavor

Understand, build, and use your social capital.

Social capital refers to the goodwill you have developed with other people. This goodwill results in other people considering you to be kind, helpful, and friendly, which creates strong relationships. The trust, reciprocity, and closeness underlying social capital can help you access information to identify opportunities, resources to exploit opportunities, and support if things go wrong.

Understand and manage your social identity.

As an entrepreneur, you have an identity based on multiple roles, such as an entrepreneur, parent, sibling, and community member. These roles can sometimes conflict, so you must manage these roles to minimize the conflict. You can establish boundaries around your different roles and rules for when one role takes precedence over another (e.g., place, time, and person). How people categorize you and your business can also reflect your identity. Your identity impacts your social motivation as an entrepreneur, how you evaluate your entrepreneurial performance, and who you compare yourself to when benchmarking your entrepreneurial performance.[1]

Form a team to create and run your venture.

Teams create more than half of all new ventures. Even solo founders tend to eventually create a team. Teams can be highly effective at under taking entrepreneurial activities, especially when team members have prior shared experience with each other. A team can provide you with a greater scope of know-how, but you need to know who knows what—who to turn to when different functions need to be performed. If you create a diverse team, you are likely to be more creative, but you also

[1] Fauchart, E., & Gruber, M. (2011). Darwinians, communitarians, and missionaries: The role of founder identity in entrepreneurship. *Academy of management journal, 54*(5), 935–957.

want to ensure some similarities across team members, such as similar ethical values.

Become and/or connect with brokers.

A broker connects previously disparate groups. If you become a broker, you can have a powerful position to benefit your venture. Alternatively, because entrepreneurs often identify opportunities without initial regard for resources, you may need to access important resources you do not have. A broker might connect you to a cluster of people with different attributes, knowledge, and resources.

Use strong ties when high trust is required and weak ties when diverse resources are needed.

Strong ties connect you to people with whom you are close, such as your family and friends. They are helpful when you need trust to advance your venture, such as initially funding your startup with money. While your friends and family are a lot like you, your weak ties are acquaintances who are often different from you and those with whom you have strong ties. Therefore, weak ties are helpful when venturing requires information and other resources that you (and your strong ties) do not possess. For example, weak ties can provide diverse, valuable information for identifying and assessing a potential opportunity.

3 Simple Rule: When It Comes to Building Relationships, Don't Always Go for What Is Easy and Natural

Look for people who are dissimilar to spice up your mind.

Building relationships with similar and nearby people is okay because it is easy and fun. These are your strong ties. They are similar to you, which is why building relationships with them is so easy. However, it would be best if you also had weak ties. Weak ties are not similar to you and are likely not located near you. Therefore, they are more challenging to find and connect with. However, they offer different information and other useful resources to develop the creativity and innovativeness needed for entrepreneurship.

Engage with dissimilar others through shared activities.

To find dissimilar others, join a sports club, a volunteer group, or a bike-riding group. These types of activities will likely connect you with more diverse people than your current friends and family. Besides, such shared activities will trigger interaction and help you develop relationships with these "different" others. Therefore, you can build strong relationships with diverse people when you find and share a common interest.

Find brokers to connect you to others.

Brokers act like bridges between two separate groups of people; they can provide the link to groups outside your current network. Expanding your network in this way can increase your access to different information and other resources critical for entrepreneurship's creative and innovative work. Consider who the brokers to diverse groups are and connect with them, perhaps by offering your services.

Become a broker.

Use your network position to make connections between two groups that are relatively disconnected from each other. For example, use your network to help people find the resources they need by linking them to people you know. Perhaps you can develop a reputation for connecting people. This can be a powerful position to hold. However, as you connect people, they may no longer need you.

4 Simple Rule: Engage Others in Dialogue Like a "Good" Professor Does in a Case Discussion

Prompt dialogue and debate to improve decision quality.

A good professor does not just lecture; they do not just tell students about their knowledge. Instead, a good professor prompts dialogue and debate about critical issues. As an entrepreneur, you will want to prompt dialogue and debate with other venture members to generate creative and innovative ideas. This dialogue and debate may create conflict, but that conflict is functional when it revolves around a task and how to execute it.

Encourage alternate viewpoints to stimulate thought.

There is little dialogue or debate about whether everyone has the same viewpoint. It would be best to tap into alternate viewpoints to create dialogue and debate. These alternate viewpoints enable venture members to explore alternatives, consider contingencies, and develop backup plans. People may be reluctant to share their alternate viewpoints. It is up to you to encourage people to express their alternate views. Indeed, people often share information that is common among those in the meeting at hand but do not share unique information—information that they have others do not have. That unique information is critical to introduce into the meeting to stimulate dialogue and debate for better decisions.

Be less interested in people having the right answer and more interested in them thinking about issues the right way.

When discussing a case, a professor might always say it is more important to think about the issue correctly than to know the case's outcome. Although students may not buy this argument, the professor emphasizes the process rather than the outcome. You can do the same. Given the uncertainty, an exemplary process does not always lead to a good outcome. However, if you focus on the process, you will receive better outcomes on average over time.

5 Simple Rule: Emphasize Inquiry with Others (Instead of Advocacy) for Generating Creative and Innovative Outcomes

Engage in conflict with curiosity.

Conflict over the nature of a task can be highly functional. Good things can happen when a team has diverse perspectives and feels comfortable sharing them within the team. These diverse perspectives can lead to dialogue and debate. Dialogue and debate can generate creative and innovative outcomes. It would be best to ensure that this task conflict does not become relationship conflict. Relationship conflict occurs when matters become of a negative personal nature. An excellent way to ensure that dialogue and debate lead to creativity rather than relationship conflict is to approach such team interactions with curiosity. Curiosity refers to an interest in understanding another person's perspective and, in this case, the nature of an entrepreneurial problem, issue, and/or response.

Encourage different opinions.

Even in highly diverse teams, team members often do not share the unique information they have that could be useful for entrepreneurial performance. Ensure you encourage people with different opinions to express their opinions to enhance task conflict for more creative and innovative solutions. It would be best to create a psychologically safe climate to encourage people with different opinions to express them. A psychologically safe climate allows people to voice information that is different from what has already been expressed and can be critical to the entrepreneurial process.

Be cognitively open and flexible.

If you approach task conflict with curiosity and passion for the process, you will be cognitively open and flexible to enable the best alternative to arise. This combination of openness and flexibility can generate highly creative and innovative outcomes. It would be best to have a diverse team and the right mindset to enable this to happen (helped by the two points above).

Use procedural fairness so people know they are valued.

If you allow people to express their opinions and consider those opinions in your decision-making process, then you offer procedural fairness. Procedural fairness is based on the process of generating task conflict and coming to a decision. You will not necessarily select team members' recommendations. Procedural fairness simply means that these individuals are an essential part of the process; they are valued, and you fully consider their opinions and other people's opinions when coming up with your decisions.

Be passionate about the process.

Although you may be interested in the outcome of your entrepreneurial team's work, it is best to focus on the process rather than the outcome. You can control and improve the process, eventually leading to good outcomes. In environments of uncertainty, the same cannot be said for a specific outcome. It may have resulted from bad luck rather than a lousy process.

6 Simple Rule: To Access Resources, Learn How to Tell a Good Story

Tell plausible stories of your entrepreneurial future.

Entrepreneurship often involves generating an idea for a potential opportunity without regard for the resources needed to exploit it. However, that does not mean resources are not necessary. It just means they need to be accessed from resource holders. To gain access, you must tell a compelling story of an envisioned future in which the focal opportunity is exploited and the desired outcomes are realized. Because it is a story about the future—abstract and hypothetical—a lot of the story's success depends on the storyteller. Learn to be an excellent storyteller to access resources and exploit opportunities.

Although it is somewhat expected, be careful telling legitimacy lies. Although your venture may lack legitimacy, all new ventures lack legitimacy (e.g., the liabilities of newness). Some entrepreneurs tell lies to make their new ventures appear more legitimate—for example, saying a venture will double in size every year, a venture is just about to sign a deal with Walmart, and a venture doesn't have any competitors. At best, resource providers dismiss such legitimacy lies as expected tactics entrepreneurs use to try to paint a rosy picture to access resources. At worst, resource providers become wary of people who tell lies regardless of how routine they are in the industry. While you should work to establish your venture's legitimacy in the story you tell, lies will not help and may harm your case. In telling your entrepreneurial story, be truthful about who you are and what you want to do. Your audience perceives this truthfulness as authenticity.

Tell an engaging story.

You can motivate your audience by offering a plausible story that makes sense, is cohesive, and offers a good roadmap to a successful outcome. The more you tell a story to yourself and others, the more feedback you receive and the more plausible your story becomes. Include your desire in the story because doing so highlights your motivation for exploiting the focal opportunity and persevering through obstacles that are likely to appear at various stages throughout the entrepreneurial process. Don't sugarcoat or tell a rosy story of your venturing so far. Talk about your adversity and how you have overcome obstacles. These struggles make your story more interesting and communicate your resilience, which will likely also be needed in the future.

Your story may need to emphasize the jockey or the horse.

Some resource holders will emphasize you (the entrepreneur, i.e., the jockey) over your venture's opportunity (i.e., the horse). These are often early stage stakeholders. They believe that many changes will occur at such an early stage and that surprises will happen. They ask themselves about you, "Can this person adapt to these unforeseen changes?" When telling a story to these investors, talk about your venture's opportunity, but realize that they will broadly assess you as the entrepreneur. Give them the information they seek in your story. Other investors will emphasize your venture's opportunity. These investors are typically involved at a later stage, when there is less uncertainty about your opportunity's attractiveness. They believe they can always replace you if your opportunity is sufficiently attractive. In such a situation, tell a story that emphasizes your venture's opportunity, development, and course corrections.

7 Simple Rule: Know Your Worth and Communicate It to Others for Effective Pricing

Don't underprice yourself.

While you may believe in yourself and your venture, you may sometimes undervalue yourself and your venture's value-added contributions. If you undervalue yourself, others will undervalue you, and your venture will not be as successful as it could have been. To improve your value, consider how a good friend would describe you to others. Take this outsider's perspective to understand your positive attributes.

Communicate the value you create for others.

With good reason, you may be reluctant to "toot your own horn" or present an inflated ego, but valuing yourself is less about these forms of boasting. At least in the entrepreneurial context, you should communicate the value your venture can establish for customers. It is not about tooting your own horn but communicating how you can serve (or help) organizations: "I want to contribute, and I think I can in the following ways."

Don't diminish or understate yourself, efforts, or outcomes.

While humility is an endearing attribute, it should not prevent you from creating a positive image and reputation for your business. Don't use language that understates your importance, venture, and market offerings. Your language communicates your worth. Using the language of venture humility is counterproductive.

8 Simple Rule: Ask for Help.

Seek help when you need it.

Seeking help is a sign of strength, not weakness. It signals that you are sufficiently self-confident and not so egotistic that you think asking for help diminishes your status in the eyes of others. Instead, asking for help means trusting the person approached, being curious to learn, and being committed to your venture's success. It also suggests that you are willing to help others when they need it through reciprocity. It can strengthen your relationship with other venture members.

Realize we all need help sometimes, which is usual in creative endeavors.

Sometimes, people face a problem and need help to resolve it but do not seek help because they are embarrassed to do so—they think it signals their incompetence. It is important to remember that everyone needs help at some stage of their work. You are not alone. Rather than becoming isolated, connect to people and help them when they need help. Your venture can establish a helping culture that strengthens cooperation with the venture.

Help the helper by sharing information about the problem or obstacle at hand.

This preparation for being helped respects the helper's time and maximizes your benefit from the interaction. Find the right person to help you. It might be someone with expertise, but it could also be a person you find trustworthy—they will not take advantage of your vulnerability.

It is also important to consider people's accessibility at the time you need help. You want a person who is accessible and has some spare time to help you in the needed way. Don't forget to thank them. They have given you time on a task not formally part of their job.

Don't worry that you are wasting their time.

This worry is a common excuse for not seeking help. However, in doing so, you may underestimate the pleasure that others receive from the prosocial activity of helping. Helping typically makes people feel good about themselves, feel stronger toward you, feel closer to your organization, and appreciate your gratitude. Besides, help involves a bond of reciprocity. They know that you will be willing to help them one day.

7

Simple Rules for Working with Cofounders

1 Simple Rule: Don't Be a Fool, Don't Rush in

Learn about your venture before adding new team members. Taking on cofounders is a fundamental decision that will substantially change your role and venture. Before taking on potential cofounders, consider the skills and competencies you need to make your venture successful. Moreover, consider your role and how you want to develop it over time. Based on an accurate understanding of yourself and your venture, develop an idea of your potential cofounders and how they should fit into your plans for your future in your venture.

These research articles provided important information in formulating the following simple rules for working with cofounders: (1) Breugst, N. (2023). *Entrepreneurial teams*. In Oxford Research Encyclopedia of Business and Management. Oxford University Press. (2) Breugst, N., Patzelt, H., & Rathgeber, P. (2015). How should we divide the pie? Equity distribution and its impact on entrepreneurial teams. *Journal of Business Venturing, 30*(1), 66–94. (3) Breugst, N., & Shepherd, D. A. (2017). If you fight with me, I'll get mad! A social model of entrepreneurial affect. *Entrepreneurship Theory and Practice, 41*(3), 379–418. (4) Breugst, N., Patzelt, H., & Shepherd, D. A. (2020). When is effort contagious in new venture management teams? Understanding the contingencies of social motivation theory.

D. A. Shepherd et al., *66 Simple Rules for Entrepreneurs*,
https://doi.org/10.1007/978-3-031-62032-4_7

Reflect on working with family members and close friends.

Many entrepreneurs primarily consider family members and close friends as potential cofounders. These potential cofounders from your network come with many benefits because you will be able to trust them and will get along well. You may also benefit from shared values that can be an excellent basis for your venture. However, before you invite cofounders from your closest circle, ask yourself if you would have invited them to join your team if you were less familiar with them. You need to identify why a specific individual is valuable for your venture and how they can contribute.

Carefully search for cofounders to maximize your overall contributions.
If you realize you cannot contribute all the skills and competencies needed in your venture, think about searching for cofounders who can complement you. You can think about your acquaintances from your current or previous jobs, college or university, and clubs or recreational activities. You may also meet potential cofounders at entrepreneurship events. However, including someone you hardly know in your founding team can be risky. Ideally, you have already had the chance to work with a potential cofounder. If not, consider agreeing on a test project in which you can determine if your working styles match.

Journal of Management Studies, 57(8), 1556–1588. (5) Breugst, N., Preller, R., Patzelt, H., & Shepherd, D. A. (2018). Information reliability and team reflection as contingencies of the relationship between information elaboration and team decision quality. *Journal of Organizational Behavior, 39*(10), 1314–1329. (6) El-Awad, Z., Brattström, A., & Breugst, N. (2022). Bridging cognitive scripts in multidisciplinary academic spinoff teams: A process perspective on how academics learn to work with non-academic managers. *Research Policy, 51*(10), 104,592. (7) Lazar, M., Miron-Spektor, E., Agarwal, R., Erez, M., Goldfarb, B., & Chen, G. (2020). Entrepreneurial team formation. *Academy of Management Annals, 14*(1), 29–59. (8) Patzelt, H., Preller, R., & Breugst, N. (2021). Understanding the life cycles of entrepreneurial teams and their ventures: An agenda for future research. *Entrepreneurship Theory and Practice, 45*(5), 1119–1153. (9) Preller, R., Patzelt, H., & Breugst, N. (2020). Entrepreneurial visions in founding teams: Conceptualization, emergence, and effects on opportunity development. *Journal of Business Venturing, 35*(2), 105914. (10) Preller, R., Breugst, N., Patzelt, H., & Dibbern, R. (2023). Team resilience building in response to co-founder exits. *Journal of Business Venturing, 38*(6), 106328. (11) Wasserman, N. (2012). *Founder's dilemmas: Anticipating and avoiding the pitfalls that can sink a startup*. Princeton University Press.

Consider the role of stakeholders in the composition of your team. You will likely have strong preferences about the individuals you want to include in your founding team and about the individuals you do not necessarily want to work with. However, other stakeholders, such as investors, may also want to shape the composition of your team. Investors often want to "professionalize" founding teams, so they may want to involve a professional manager in your team or reduce your or your cofounders' managerial responsibilities. These situations can be challenging at both a professional and a personal level. Think about and discuss these scenarios before you start to collaborate with investors. An important question for you is do you want to (a) build a bigger pie and get a smaller slice of it (i.e., lose control for personal wealth) or (b) have a larger slice of a smaller pie (i.e., less wealth to maintain personal control).

2 Simple Rule: Make Sure to Invest Time in Setting up Your Founding Team

Do not always prioritize your team's work over working on your team.
When you start to work together in your founding team, you will likely face high time pressure and be confronted with many urgent tasks. In such a situation, you risk investing all your time in operational tasks and strategic decision-making without devoting sufficient time to setting up your team for successful collaboration. Make sure to find time to discuss your expectations and preferences for your venture and founding team. You can find many resources online, such as questions to ask cofounders.[1] These resources can help you better understand your cofounders' ideas and build a solid basis for your collaboration.

Rely on cofounder agreements and contracts to build up your team. Working together in a newly established entrepreneurial team is challenging because you may not know enough about the other team

[1] You can find an example of a list of 50 questions to discuss with your cofounders here: https://founderhandbook.org/management/50-questions-to-explore-with-a-potential-co-founder.

members and how well you will be able to work together. You can explicitly write down your expectations for each other and your venture to reduce this uncertainty. These cofounder agreements and contracts can guide how you and your cofounders are expected to behave. For example, you can specify how you want to make strategic decisions, what happens if a team member does not meet expectations, and how you want to organize your venture. Many entrepreneurship centers have legal experts who can help you refine these agreements and contracts, customizing them for your precise requirements.

Think carefully about how to split equity among your team.
There is no easy formula for splitting equity among your founding team. Different cofounders may attach different price tags to different contributions. While you may overvalue your contributions, your cofounders may overvalue theirs. Listen to your cofounders' perspectives and ensure that yours is heard. For the positive development of your team, you must agree on a split that all members of your founding team consider fair.

Consider dynamic equity splits.
The contributions you and your cofounders make to your venture will only become evident over time. These future-oriented nature of these contributions are even more challenging when deciding on your equity split. However, you do not necessarily have to agree on a fixed split in the early days of your venture. Instead, you can rely on vesting schemes specifying that all team members will need to earn their equity stakes over time, perhaps by achieving specified milestones. These vesting schemes can include so-called cliffs, which define criteria for when founding team members are entitled to harvest their equity stakes, for example, when they have stayed one year in the venture.

3 Simple Rule: If You Want Your Founding Team to Function Well, Nurture It

Work with your teammates' visions even if they do not match yours.

Sharing a vision with your fellow founding team members can be motivating because a shared vision provides a strong direction for the team. However, sharing a vision can be challenging, especially when other members have different and varied opinions on what the team should be doing and how it should be accomplished. In this case, you may have different perspectives and want to follow different paths to develop your venture. This variety may make you more flexible because you can pursue different opportunities, but you must ensure your team works as a cohesive unit—everyone on the same page—with professionalism. You must deal with the complexity of integrating different perspectives, visions, and activities with high professionalism.

Motivate each other in the team.
Entrepreneurs often assume that founding team members inspire each other and that motivation is contagious in such teams. However, hard work is not always reciprocated in teams—a hard-working team member can also signal to peers that their effort is not needed anymore. If you want to create a climate in which your motivation is contagious, make sure to put your team in focus. Your team members should develop the feeling that all of you sit in the same boat because it is up to all of you to prevent your venture from failing and defend it against harsh competition. It is under such conditions that team members' effort is most contagious.

Share the exclusive information each team member holds.
When you only focus on your information, you may make low-quality decisions because your individual information can be misleading. In your discussions, you need to make sure all information from all members of the founding team is accessible to the team. However, the exclusive information possessed by individual team members is often largely ignored in discussions because teams tend to focus on what they already

know. Thus, try to make exclusive and potentially valuable information more salient by highlighting the new insights you gain in team meetings. Call out members with unique information and share this information with the team. If others do the same, then your founding team can make creative and/or superior decisions. Reflect jointly on how these new insights shape your perspectives on the decisions you need to make. Note the triggers that encouraged team members to reveal their unique information.

Take time to reflect jointly on your teamwork and your decision-making process.
While it is essential to get work done and to make decisions in your founding team, you should, as a team, take some time to reflect on how you work together and how you make decisions. When your team reviews how you work together, you can adapt your team processes and goals. This adaptation can help you improve your teamwork and better use the information available to your team. Moreover, team reflection is constructive in unpredictable environments because it can help you make essential modifications in the face of change. The end of a project is an ideal time to reflect on the decision-making and teamwork on that project to understand what went well, what went poorly, and what could have been done better. However, such reflection does not have to occur only at the end of a project and can be effectively engaged as a pause in an ongoing decision-making process.

4 Simple Rule: Make Sure Your Team Can Manage Team Issues

Introduce clear rules for your communication, ideally before you experience team issues.
Your journey as a team can become burdensome. Sometimes, you are unsatisfied with your teammates' performance, and they will be unhappy with yours. Think about ways to give each other constructive feedback that helps each team member grow from difficult situations and collectively improve your team. Explaining your concerns is helpful; blaming

is not. It is most effective if you try to develop some ideas about how you could behave in a similar situation in the future. You have to learn to work and communicate with each other.

Learn that not all conflict is dysfunctional.
Conflict in your founding team is unavoidable. However, some of this conflict has the potential to advance your venture. Distinguish between relationship conflict, which refers to tensions between people and clashes of personalities, and task conflict, which refers to disagreements on viewpoints or procedures. While relationship conflict can harm your venture (through the destruction of personal relationships), task conflict can improve your team's decision quality and benefit your venture (by raising diverse perspectives and information). Allow your team to have such task conflict, but if you realize it's getting too intense, take a break and calm down to avoid transitioning from task conflict to relationship conflict. Keep conflict focused on work, not people.

Reduce the negative effect of dysfunctional conflict.
Sometimes, dysfunctional relationship conflict may occur in the busy daily grind of your venture. While you might be annoyed or hurt by a cofounder's behavior, think about the situation your cofounder is in. For example, they might have shown more aggressive behavior because of the pressure or high workload they are experiencing. Indeed, searching for explanations for your cofounders' behavior will help you be less affected by conflict. Keep emotions in balance; avoid overidentifying with them or escalating negative emotions into a bigger problem than necessary.

Think about your role in conflict.
It is often easy to blame your cofounders for conflict, but this will not help you or your team progress. Think about your role in conflict and reflect on your biases. Situations can be interpreted differently depending on people's perspectives. Try to take your cofounders' perspectives explicitly; you may also reach out to others who can make your cofounders' perspectives more accessible. Thinking about conflict from several perspectives may help you cope with it better and resolve the underlying problem.

5 Simple Rule: Your Team May Not Stay Together, but a Breakup Doesn't Have to Be a Disaster

Think about founding team breakups before they happen.
We have already highlighted the benefits of contracts for setting up a team. Contracts can also protect you and your venture when a cofounder wants to leave the venture. Speak about potential exit scenarios before any team member has started to think about an exit. What will you do if a team member comes across a more attractive opportunity? What will you do if you think that one team member is underperforming? Do you want to agree on specific buyout terms? While there are no easy and general answers to questions like these, thinking about them in advance can help avoid a complete disaster.

Founding team breakups can be painful. Get external help.
Founding team breakups are highly emotional. Your feelings and your cofounders' feelings are probably hurt. In these troubled situations, staying professional and making rational decisions about your venture are hard. Try to find somebody who can take a more neutral perspective on the situation to provide an external view. This external view can help you to distance yourself from the emotions arising from the exit and distinguish between venture-related and personal challenges. Also, consider involving a mediator or a coach in the negotiations with your cofounders. An impartial professional may reduce useless fights that drain your energy without resulting in any solution.

Prevent reputational damage by agreeing on an exit story.
A hostile founding team breakup can damage the reputation of your team members, your venture, and current stakeholders. Investors may be reluctant to invest in your venture or your future projects when they are skeptical about team stability. To prevent this reputational damage, it can be helpful to develop an exit story that all cofounders can agree about. In this story, you present plausible reasons for the team breakup, reducing reputational damage for all concerned. Sharing a consistent story with all your stakeholders can prevent or at least reduce reputational damage

compared to a hostile breakup where all parties wash their dirty laundry in public.

Use a breakup in your founding team to make you stronger. While a team member exit can be challenging, successfully dealing with the exit can have positive consequences for your venture. When you digest the exit, you need to rethink your venture. It would be best to deal with the outflow of resources and the specific skills and competencies the exiting cofounder contributed. Moreover, it would be best to redistribute the responsibilities among the remaining founding team members. In this process, you may be able to set up your venture in a way that is more resilient to future changes in the founding team and to better react to unforeseen changes in the venture environment. Also, if you start a new venture, this experience can help you craft useful contracts with your cofounders and even build a venture that depends less on the individual cofounders.

8

Simple Rules for Managing Employees

1 Simple Rule: Consider the People You Can Attract to Your Startup

Consider employing those who have worked for new ventures before. The startup environment is dynamic, uncertain, and often stressful, requiring specific skills from your employees. When hiring someone new,

---

These research articles provided important information in formulating the following simple rules for managing employees: (1) Amabile, T., Fisher, C. M., & Pillemer, J. (2014). IDEO's Culture of Helping. *Harvard Business Review, 92*(1), 54–61. (2) Breugst, N., Domurath, A., Patzelt, H., & Klaukien, A. (2012). Perceptions of entrepreneurial passion and employees' commitment to entrepreneurial ventures. *Entrepreneurship: Theory & Practice, 36*(1), 171–192. (3) Domurath, A., Taggar, S., & Patzelt, H. (2023). A contingency model of employees' turnover intent in young ventures. *Small Business Economics*, forthcoming. (4) Farson, R., & Keyes, R. (2006). The failure-tolerant leader. *Managing Innovation and Change, 249*. (5) Patzelt, H., Gartzia, L., Wolfe, M., & Shepherd, D. A. (2021). Managing negative emotions from entrepreneurial project failure: When and how does supportive leadership help employees? *Journal of Business Venturing, 36*(5), 106128. (6) Roach, M., & Sauermann, H. (2015). Founder or joiner? The role of preferences and context in shaping different entrepreneurial interests. *Management Science, 61*(9), 2160–2184. (7) Sauermann, H. (2018). Fire in the belly? Employee motives and innovative performance in start-ups versus established firms. *Strategic Entrepreneurship Journal, 12*(4), 423–454. (8) Van Lancker, E., Knockaert, M., Collewaert, V., & Breugst, N. (2023). Preparing for scaling: A study on founder role evolution. *Journal of Business Venturing, 38*(4), 106315.

D. A. Shepherd et al., *66 Simple Rules for Entrepreneurs*,
https://doi.org/10.1007/978-3-031-62032-4_8

look for those who know the startup environment. These employees are likely to cope with the demands of a quickly changing environment and stay on board even if times are tough (as they sometimes are for every startup).

Look for Jacks- and Jills-of-all-trades.

Just as the startup environment changes quickly, so will the tasks your employees have to do. In such a situation, it can be advantageous if your employees have a more general skillset rather than a highly specialized skill set. That way, you can allocate them to new tasks during venture development that you could not foresee when hiring.

Giving up some of the control over your venture can be challenging.

Many entrepreneurs describe their ventures as their babies. They highlight their close bonds to their ventures and their level of dedication. Still, you may not be able to work on all the tasks required to run your venture on your own, and—sooner or later—you will likely need to hire employees to support you. Metaphorically, they may become babysitters of your venture. Ensure you communicate your expectations concerning your overall idea of your venture and highlight the values important to you. However, consider the autonomy of your employees so they will feel sufficiently responsible for the venture (or at least their venture tasks). They may become crucial to further developing your venture when they can make suggestions and incorporate their ideas.

2 Simple Rule: You Will Shape Your Employees, but They Will also Shape You

It is great if you are passionate, but be aware of what you signal to employees.

When you display your entrepreneurial passion, employees can catch fire from you and invest more effort into your venture. However, be aware that different signals can impact employee motivation differently. Suppose you display that you are passionate about developing your venture's product and making the venture successful. That is great because it signals to employees that you are putting great effort into the current venture. However, this can backfire if you signal that you are passionate about founding ventures more generally. Employees may fear that you are already looking for the next venture to found and that you are thus less committed to the growth and scaling of the current one.

Empower employees to craft their tasks and roles.

Employees will likely come up with suggestions on how they will perform their tasks and perhaps even which tasks they should perform. Because your employees will become experts in their assigned roles, they will likely have relevant insights into these roles and make meaningful suggestions to improve them. If these suggestions fit your ideas of how your venture should work, they can be invaluable to make the venture more efficient. Employees willing to assume more responsibility may even take over some of your tasks and reduce your workload; you can then reallocate your attention to other critical issues.

Guide employees in building your venture's culture.

Beyond their regular tasks, employees may also develop some informal roles in your venture. For example, employees may come up with some rituals for your venture or organize events for venture members. If these activities are consistent with your values and ideas for your venture, supporting and encouraging them makes sense. In this way, your employees can become the ideal spreaders of your venture's values and help you build its culture as it grows.

When your employees' projects fail, help them get over it early.
Projects in new ventures often fail, creating negative emotions in employees that impact their learning and motivation. However, you can help your employees get over these emotions. In particular, provide them with emotional support and tell them that failure can happen to anyone; indeed, failure may be positive if they learn from it. Such support efforts are particularly effective soon after a failure event occurs.

3 Simple Rule: Build a Culture in Which Your Employees Thrive

Establish cooperation within your venture rather than competition.

Although competition can bring out the best in individuals (or groups versus other groups), it can limit information sharing across competing units. Information sharing and learning are critical for venture progress when dealing with an uncertain environment. Rather than stimulate a competitive spirit, it is better to stimulate cooperation and collaboration. Create a culture where venture members help each other perform their essential tasks to enhance innovation and member satisfaction.

When helping someone learn, engage actively in listening to understand the underlying issue.

Active listening helps you better understand to offer more effective help. Active listening does not mean that you remain quiet. It can involve asking probing questions to understand the situation better. The person asking for help is making themselves vulnerable to you (admitting they do not have the answers), so show respect to them in how you deal with their vulnerability. Remember, everyone needs some help sometimes. Over and above demonstrating your trustworthiness, let people know you are accessible. If you signal you are too busy, people will not approach you for help. These signals of unapproachability can diminish the helping culture and adversely impact your venture's innovativeness.

Promote a helping culture by providing slack and discretion.
Help requires venture members to have some slack time to help others on a task not formally allocated to them. They need to believe they have sufficient time to perform their tasks and some spare time to help others with their tasks. To be effective, help needs to be a voluntary endeavor. You need to give venture members the discretion of when, who, and how they help.

4 Simple Rule: If You Want to Be Entrepreneurial, You Need to Be a Failure-Tolerant Leader

Eliminate or minimize an anti-failure bias in your venture.
You need to realize that people try to hide their mistakes and failures. When they do so, your venture loses an excellent opportunity to learn. It would be best to create an organizational culture where people feel comfortable revealing the activities that led to a failure and enabling your venture to learn. Ironically, if your venture has an anti-failure bias, failures will be more costly.

Display empathy.
Empathy means that you can understand and share a person's emotional and cognitive experiences. As a failure-tolerant leader, you can build empathy with other venture members by explaining how you have experienced failures, how you felt when a failure occurred, and what you did to learn from those experiences that eventually led to success. Such empathy signals communicate to venture members that failures are accepted as part of the entrepreneurial process. It may be tough to tell stories of your failures, but it builds credibility, displays courage, and promotes a creative and innovative climate within your venture.

Show interest in members' processes.

Interest in members' processes signals to venture members that processes are essential and that outcomes do not always reflect a good process. Be curious about how venture members start projects, how they are progressing, what issues they are facing, how they are addressing those issues, and so on. The added advantage of showing interest in members' processes is that it can help facilitate their intrinsic motivation, which is critical to creativity.

Emphasize collaboration rather than competition.

While competition can generate energy for improving performance on specific tasks, collaboration is more critical in creative endeavors. Collaboration encourages venture members to share information throughout the organization, enhancing creativity and innovativeness.

Tolerate failures that enhance learning; don't tolerate other failures.

Not all failures are tolerable. Tolerable failures are well thought-out, provide an opportunity to learn, and are diligently performed. Intolerable failures are ill-conceived, provide little learning, or are based on negligence. To state the obvious, you must tolerate tolerable failures but not intolerable ones.

9

Simple Rules for Growing Your Venture

1 Simple Rule: Growth Is a Challenging Journey; Be Well Prepared

Plan early to leverage your team's competencies.

When your venture enters a growth phase, you will face many challenges, such as expanding production, increasing marketing activities, coping with enhanced customer interactions, and managing more

---

These research articles provided important information in formulating the following simple rules for growing your ventures: (1) Earley, P. C., & Mosakowski, E. (2004). Cultural intelligence. *Harvard Business Review, 82*(10), 139–146. (2) Garvin, D. A., Edmondson, A. C., & Gino, F. (2008). Is yours a learning organization? *Harvard Business Review, 86*(3), 109–116. (3) Greiner, L. E. (1972). Evolution and revolution as organisations grow. *Harvard Business Review, 50*(4), 37–46. (4) Shepherd, D. A., Breugst, N., & Patzelt, H. (2023). A founding-team model of creating a venture's culture. *Journal of Business Venturing, 38*(2), 106286. (5) Tryba, A., Patzelt, H., & Breugst, N. (2023). Knowledge diversity and venture growth: The contingent effects of early planning and experimentation. *British Journal of Management, 34*(1), 343–362. (6) Wiklund, J., Patzelt, H., & Shepherd, D. A. (2009). Building an integrative model of small business growth. *Small Business Economics, 32*(4), 351–374. (7) Wiklund, J., & Shepherd, D. A. (2005). Entrepreneurial orientation and small business performance: A configurational approach. *Journal of Business Venturing, 20*, 71–91.

D. A. Shepherd et al., *66 Simple Rules for Entrepreneurs*,
https://doi.org/10.1007/978-3-031-62032-4_9

complex financials. However, even if you have the required competencies on your team, those competencies must be well coordinated to facilitate growth. Early planning can help you coordinate the diverse competencies on your team and ensure they are used in the best way for expanding your venture.

Experiment, but not without a plan.

You can experiment with different approaches to find the right way to grow. This approach is fine, but it may not automatically work out. A team with diverse competencies and—importantly—a plan is also required for success. A plan helps you coordinate your teams' competencies and the information generated from your various growth experiments. Try to develop all three—experimentation, team knowledge diversity, and an early plan—in parallel to maximize your venture's growth.

Adopt an entrepreneurial strategic posture.

Particularly in environments where technologies and customer demands change quickly, ventures with an entrepreneurial strategic posture often grow more quickly than those that do not have such a posture. An entrepreneurial strategic posture is proactive, risk-taking, and innovative. If you integrate these three principles into your strategic decision-making, you may outgrow your competitors quickly.

Be aware that you will need a lot of resources, and be creative when accessing them.

Growth is resource-intensive. To grow successfully, it would be best to build new production plants, acquire new talent, expand your marketing activities, and build new distribution channels. The good news is, however, that you may not need to do all these things by yourself. A strategic alliance can help you access some of these resources. Allying with large companies can provide access to their marketing and distribution capabilities, saving resources and enhancing success on your growth trajectory. Joining forces with other ventures to set up a new production facility or a research and development facility can save you money and provide access to talent. Identify such possibilities upfront to allocate your venture's growth resources most efficiently.

2 Simple Rule: Transform Your Venture Multiple Times

When creativity does not move your venture forward anymore, select a leader.

In the early phase, you may feel excited that everyone in your venture can work on the tasks they like and be creative in executing them. Coordination is informal, and communication is frequent. However, a creativity-driven approach becomes challenging as you take on more employees. Not everyone can coordinate and communicate with everyone else anymore, leading to double work and inefficiencies. To overcome this situation, select a leader (yourself or someone else) who assigns clear responsibilities to venture members, introduces new communication channels and business processes, and allocates resources. These practices can provide the way into the next growth phase.

If you feel overwhelmed, foster delegation.

Although you may take your venture to a new level with further growth, it is likely that over time, you will become overwhelmed by the complexity and multitude of decisions you have to make. In addition, people in lower-level managerial positions who emerged as a growth consequence may feel frustrated by the need to coordinate their decisions with you. These people may ultimately leave your venture. To overcome this situation, establish delegation structures and empower lower-level managers for further growth.

When your venture becomes too complex, formalize your systems.

To grow your venture, you may have added increasingly more products, entered diverse markets, created multiple units within the venture, and provided individualized incentives. All this creates complexity, making it difficult to oversee your venture. Therefore, at this point, your organization should be formalized. This means that you may combine and/or merge some products and units, reassess whether all markets served are worth the effort or if focusing on the most profitable ones is a better solution, and introduce a formal incentive system that applies across the organization. This may also include expanding the central administration at your company's headquarters.

To keep venture units entrepreneurial, spin them off.

Some units within ventures, like startups, may need creativity when developing highly innovative technologies or products. Consider giving them autonomy. They can become independent ventures with you retaining a major stake, or they can be ventures within your firm, for example, centers of excellence with high decision latitude and the possibility to do business their way.

3 Simple Rule: Build Your Cultural Intelligence to Enter Foreign Markets

Recognize that doing business in other countries is common for entrepreneurs.

With internet platforms and other communication mechanisms, many entrepreneurial firms target international customers and obtain supplies from international sources. Some new ventures are created with international markets in mind and are born global. Be open to taking your business to other countries.

Build your cultural intelligence.

Cultural intelligence means you can distinguish someone's behavior by categorizing it as distinctive to that person, consistent with a particular national culture, or something that all people do. Correctly making these categorizations helps you better understand the person you are dealing with. It can also help you understand when knowledge about interactions with a person is transferable to others from the same culture and when such generalizations are inappropriate.

Use your head to build cultural intelligence.

You can build your cultural intelligence by thinking about people's behavior. You can suspend judgment when assessing someone's behavior to determine if it is cultural or idiosyncratic. You can improve your thinking by role-playing activities to learn about cultural activities. You can also use other learning strategies to learn about other cultures, such as reading books and watching instructional videos.

Use your body to build cultural intelligence.

You can build cultural intelligence by adopting some of the habits of the culture you want to learn about. This adoption can help you understand and generate trust with people from that culture. Don't go too far in imitating certain behaviors—it may come across as mocking them and/or as being inauthentic. Stay within the bounds of your authenticity and make minor changes to your habits to reflect the cultural context.

Use your heart to build cultural intelligence.

You can build cultural intelligence by being motivated to better prepare for cross-cultural interactions. Also, you can build self-efficacy by succeeding in initial cross-cultural interactions. Cultural self-efficacy means that you believe you can be successful at cross-control interactions, enabling you to persevere in such situations and achieve success. To build this self-efficacy, engage in a few minor activities that will give you a chance to be successful—to have a few small wins. Then, you can build toward greater cross-cultural challenges.

Use your network to build cultural intelligence.

Search your network to determine if you know people from the focal culture. These people may provide you with critical information about the culture. They may also provide an ideal opportunity for cross-cultural role-play in a psychologically safe environment—an excellent opportunity to learn at a low cost of failure.

To learn a culture, immerse yourself in it.
Immersion requires your head, heart, and body to thoroughly and actively understand your environment. Take away your cultural support from home and dive into the new culture. Experts say the best way to learn a language is to immerse yourself in a context where only that language is used. You have no choice but to learn.

4 Simple Rule: To Make Your Organization Entrepreneurial, Enhance Its Capacity to Learn

Learn from feedback to adapt.
When facing a dynamic environment, your venture's initial alignment with the environment can be lost—your approach is likely consistent with the past but not the present conditions. You can't anticipate all the environmental changes in advance. Still, you can try to notice them when they happen, learn from your venture's outcomes in this new environment, and respond by adapting the venture to be aligned with the environment again. This adaption requires you and your venture to learn from feedback from the venture's actions. Be open to feedback about conditions that have changed.

Focus on learning for venture dynamism.
A dynamic capability is a capability that can change a venture's routines and systems. Learning is the ultimate dynamic capability. By learning from your venture's actions, you can change your capabilities to regain alignment with the environment, which will in turn be reflected in enhanced venture performance. Therefore, learning is a capability that can help drive changes in existing capabilities and the development of new capabilities.

Offer psychological safety.

Psychological safety is an attribute of a venture's climate that allows members to share information, including novel ideas, without being denigrated by others. This information-sharing among venture members is critical to creating new knowledge and spreading excellence throughout an organization. Psychological safety is paramount in learning from failure. When you feel psychologically safe to share information about your contribution to a failed project, you and others can learn from that failure. However, when psychological safety is lacking, people will hide mistakes and failures, and important sources of learning are wasted.

Recruit and promote diversity.

Diverse venture members can provide different sources of information and perspectives on the same event or task. Encouraging this diversity provides greater scope for your venture to learn and can thus improve creativity and innovation.

Schedule some pauses so you have a chance to reflect.

Entrepreneurs often move quickly. Speed is good. However, occasionally, you need to pause and reflect on what has happened to give your brain a chance to catch up and learn. Learning is not automatic or instantaneous. You may move quickly in the wrong direction without pausing to allow for reflection. Reflection is necessary for course corrections.

5 Simple Rule: Formalize Some of Your Personality to Build Your Venture's Culture

Use your personality to build your venture's culture.

A culture for a venture is critical for managing members to ensure they have shared values, beliefs, and assumptions that generate organizational behaviors. While established ventures have an organizational culture, you must build and establish one when you create a new venture. That organizational culture will likely reflect your personality as an entrepreneur because the venture is created to fulfill your goals and desires.

Provide a clear vision.
A vision conceptualizes what you want your venture to look like. Communicating this vision within the venture is essential because it ensures that all members adopt the same values, providing purpose to their activities. With shared values and an understanding of the venture's purpose, venture members can cooperate, coordinate, and collectively generate superior decisions, learning, and performance.

Tell stories, highlight artifacts, and document systems.
While your personality can influence venture members' behaviors, you need to establish a culture that can work for an extended period and as your venture grows. You can convert your personality to an organizational culture by articulating the values, beliefs, and assumptions that underlie your venture. Once the organizational culture has been articulated, you can start codifying it. Codification means documenting the aspects of the organizational culture. For example, some entrepreneurs write about their organizational culture as a manifesto. For the culture to work, it needs to be shared by all members. Such sharing can be facilitated by telling stories and displaying artifacts and other symbols that reflect the culture.

Recruit and train the "right" people to fit the venture's culture.
You can maintain the organizational culture as your venture grows by recruiting the right people. By "right," we mean people who fit with the current organizational culture or people you are confident are willing to adopt it. Whether for recruits or established members, it is essential that your training involves reinforcing the organizational culture, such as telling stories and highlighting artifacts that reflect the venture's underlying values, beliefs, and assumptions.

Recognize that your venture's culture can be a source of competitive advantage.
A strong and widely shared organizational culture can give your venture several competitive advantages. Your venture's culture is unique

because it is based on your personality and has evolved based on the venture's various encounters. This uniqueness makes the organizational culture a source of competitive advantage that is difficult for others to imitate.

Build your venture's culture in conjunction with organizational capabilities.

While an organizational culture can provide numerous benefits to a venture, the venture must be able to back it up. A venture with a culture but no capabilities is like having the sizzle without the steak.

Don't outgrow your venture's culture.

You may desire your venture to grow as rapidly as possible, but rapid growth has some dangers. Often, growth is enabled by a venture's organizational culture. However, growth can stretch the organizational culture too far such that the venture loses its "essence." Recognizing the limits of your organizational culture and the strains growth puts on it is essential. It may be wise to grow only as fast as your ability to maintain your venture's culture.

10

Simple Rules for Riding the Emotional Roller Coaster

1 Simple Rule: Don't Ignore Your Negative Emotions

Fear does not have to stop you, shift your focus to essential details.

These research articles provided important information in formulating the following simple rules for riding the emotional roller coaster: (1) Cacciotti, G., Hayton, J. C., Mitchell, J. R., & Giazitzoglu, A. (2016). A reconceptualization of fear of failure in entrepreneurship. *Journal of Business Venturing, 31*(3), 302–325. (2) Druskat, V. U., & Wolff, S. B. (2001). Building the emotional intelligence of groups. *Harvard Business Review, 79*(3), 80–91. (3) Gasper, K., & Clore, G. L. (2002). Attending to the big picture: Mood and global versus local processing of visual information. *Psychological Science, 13*(1), 34–40. (4) Goleman, D., & Boyatzis, R. (2017). Emotional intelligence has 12 elements. Which do you need to work on? *Harvard Business Review, 84*(2), 1–5. (5) Kammerlander, N., & Breugst, N. (2019). Construals matter: Painting the big picture or drawing the brushstrokes of the family firm. *Family Business Review, 32*(3), 222–232. (6) Tacke, F., Knockaert, M., Patzelt, H., & Breugst, N. (2023). When do greedy entrepreneurs exhibit unethical pro-organizational behavior? The role of new venture team trust. *Journal of Management, 49*(3), 974–1004. (7) Warnick, B. J., Murnieks, C. Y., McMullen, J. S., & Brooks, W. T. (2018). Passion for entrepreneurship or passion for the product? A conjoint analysis of angel and VC decision-making. *Journal of Business Venturing, 33*(3), 315–332.

D. A. Shepherd et al., *66 Simple Rules for Entrepreneurs*,
https://doi.org/10.1007/978-3-031-62032-4_10

Fear of failure can stop people from taking action. However, fear can also make you more aware of potential challenges that may come up during your journey. Indeed, fear helps you look for details that can go wrong and determine if your idea is feasible. So, you are probably better prepared for the entrepreneurial journey if you listen to your fear and protect yourself against the negative outcomes you worry about. However, while fear is excellent for focusing on details, don't forget to allow more positive emotions to surface because they will allow you to look at your venture holistically. Balancing negative and positive emotions can help you see broad ideas and specific aspects of your venture.

Use your negative emotions for information.

Every venture can experience difficult times, which can create negative emotions. Although nobody wants to feel bad, be sensitive to your negative emotions and do not ignore them. They may entail important information about aspects of your venture that are currently not performing as expected. As you try to understand your negative emotions, you may also come to understand what you need to improve to bring your venture back on track again.

Your negative emotions tell you what you need as a person.

Negative emotions also hold necessary signals for you. If you feel frustrated and mad, think about the potential sources of these emotions. Do you have the impression that your outcomes do not match your inputs? Do you think others (or life more generally) treat you unfairly? Do you feel overwhelmed by your workload? All these negative emotions may be valid—at least to a certain extent. They can tell you that you need to take a break from your venture, that you need to talk to a cofounder or an employee, or that you should try to renegotiate some agreements. While it can make sense to postpone important decisions until your negative emotions have subsided, negative emotions represent essential pointers to the decisions you should make and the urgency of those decisions.

Greed may motivate you, but rely on social control to avoid escalation.

Being "hungry" and "wanting more" can positively affect entrepreneurs and inspire them to invest high effort. However, if you realize that you experience greed, you should think about the feelings triggered by greed. These feelings can be challenging to control and can potentially escalate into behaviors that put your venture (and you) at risk. Consider relying on social control mechanisms, such as highly competent cofounders or investors monitoring your venture, to avoid negative consequences while potentially enjoying the motivation from greed.

2 Simple Rule: Running a Venture Can Be Exhausting, So Make Sure You Manage Your Entrepreneurial Energy Right

Make sure you have enough energy to build your venture and ensure well-being.

Most entrepreneurs will tell you that building a venture can be exhausting. Your personal energy level is one of the most critical resources for successfully navigating the ups and downs of the entrepreneurial journey. While building a venture can be energizing, the journey's high uncertainty, workload, resource constraints, and potential setbacks can severely deplete your energy. Monitor your energy levels and ensure they are sufficiently high for the challenging future.

Balance tasks that are energy draining with those that are energy fueling.

We all get more energy from some tasks than from others. Collecting positive customer feedback can fuel your energy, while talking to unsatisfied investors can drain your energy. Make sure you balance both tasks to maintain sufficient energy in your reservoir. Consider involving your cofounders more if you feel too many tasks are energy draining rather than energy fueling.

Be aware of the promises you make to yourself and others.

When building your venture, you make promises to yourself and others (cofounders, employees, investors, customers, collaboration partners) regarding what you and your venture can do. Successfully delivering on these promises can be energy fueling and provide key motivation for you. However, sometimes, you cannot fulfill what you have promised yourself, and such failures can drain your energy and lead to disillusionment with the venture. Make sure you that you make realistic promises (to self and others) and renegotiate them if they become unrealistic.

If your energy is draining, take a break from your venture to avoid fatigue.

Some entrepreneurs experience decreasing work motivation, lack of concentration, and an unhealthy sleep schedule. These can all signal that your energy is already at a low level; they signal you need a break. When this happens, try to participate in activities outside your venture more intensely. Engage in your hobbies, spend more time with your family and friends, or go on holiday. In most cases, these activities will be sufficient to recharge your batteries. Most importantly, get quality sleep—go to a sleep doctor if this is an issue. Work problems are magnified when you do not sleep enough the night before.

When you feel fatigued, turn to your venture members.

If your energy level has become too low or empty, distracting yourself from your venture is often insufficient to regain energy to work on it again. You are experiencing entrepreneurial fatigue—a persistent lack of energetic activation for building your venture. In this case, discuss your situation with your cofounders or mentors and ask them for support. Further, look out for positive signals indicating that some aspects of your venture are going well. You may not be able to fulfill all the promises you made, but you will likely be able to keep some—and perhaps more than you thought in the first place.

3 Simple Rule: Follow Your Entrepreneurial Passion

Passion can be the basis of your venture.

Many entrepreneurs highlight the relevance of passion for their ventures. You can be passionate about a specific product or problem, and your passion for working on it can ignite your entrepreneurial spirit. As an entrepreneur, you can also be passionate about specific activities that entrepreneurs engage in, such as tinkering with new ideas, setting up a venture, or nurturing your growing firm. Thinking about activities or topics you are passionate about is an excellent basis for starting a venture.

Considering activities you are passionate about, is the ideal career advice.

Entrepreneurs can be passionate about different activities and roles in their ventures. You might realize that some activities make you feel good while others don't. For example, some entrepreneurs enjoy setting up a new venture but become bored when the venture grows and becomes more stable. Awareness of your feelings can help you make decisions for your entrepreneurial career. You can design your role(s) to align with your passion. If you mainly enjoy setting up ventures, you may want to think about a good time to exit your current venture and start a new one, becoming a serial entrepreneur. You may also be the person who is passionate about continuously developing and improving new products. In this case, it can be helpful to search for a cofounder who is passionate about nurturing your venture when it starts growing.

Be passionate, but ensure it is harmonious, not obsessive.

Harmonious passion is when a person engages in an activity because it is connected to who they are and generates positive emotions. Harmonious passion for the entrepreneurial journey can provide the energy necessary to drive the creativity process for an extended period. In contrast, a person is obsessively passionate about a task if they feel obliged to work on it to avoid negative consequences. Obsessive passion may initially provide the energy to work on your venture, but it is rarely sustainable. You may hear stories about entrepreneurs who are obsessively passionate about their ventures such that they work 20-hour days, seven days a week. If you become obsessively passionate where your self-worth is tied to the value of your venture, then other aspects of your life will deteriorate, and you may even burn out. In contrast, following your harmonious passion can help you find a path that gives you personal fulfillment and can thus help refuel your energy.

4 Simple Rule: Build Your Emotional Intelligence

Develop your emotional intelligence of self.

Develop your understanding of your emotions—how you feel in different situations—and develop some capabilities to regulate those emotions. Reflecting on past events can increase your emotional intelligence. You can also improve your emotional intelligence by gaining honest feedback from people who know you well.

Develop your emotional intelligence of others.

Develop your understanding of how others experience emotions and why they experience these emotions and be able to help them regulate their emotional reactions. Again, you can develop your emotional intelligence of others by reflecting on your interpersonal interactions and gaining feedback from those people. After an event, ask them how they felt and how you could have helped their emotional responses.

Deliver and receive honest feedback about emotions.

This emotional information exchange can help you improve your emotional intelligence, and your interaction partner can improve their emotional intelligence as well. This exchange can help strengthen your relationship with them. Indeed, having emotionally intelligent friends is a great asset. However, you have to be open to receiving honest feedback, which might be challenging sometimes. Similarly, delivering feedback to others about their emotional responses may also be challenging, but the benefits can be great.

Generate positive emotions to think creatively.

Positive emotions can increase your attentional awareness and cognitive capabilities for thinking creatively and generating innovations critical for the entrepreneurial process. You can also improve your entrepreneurial performance and feel more satisfied at work by generating positive emotions in yourself and your colleagues. Generate positive emotions (in yourself and others) to think creatively.

Build your emotional intelligence to enhance your job performance and satisfaction.

To perform well at entrepreneurial tasks, it is essential to regulate your emotions and the emotions of others. By improving your emotional intelligence, you can improve your entrepreneurial performance and help others regulate their emotions for improved performance. Regulating your emotions, improving entrepreneurial performance, and helping others perform better can make you more satisfied with your entrepreneurial career and life.

5 Simple Rule: Pursue Moderate Stress at Work to Enhance Life

Realize stress is an appraisal.

Stress results from your assessment of a situation and your concern that you do not have sufficient resources to address that situation or threat. Stress may be grounded in the facts of the situation. Still, it is also important to realize that it is your interpretation and assessment of the situation (vis-à-vis your capabilities and coping skills) that cause stress rather than the objective situation itself.

Stress means something important is at stake.

You do not feel stressed about events that are not relevant to you. You feel stress when facing challenging situations that are important to you. Telling yourself that stress signals the importance of a situation for you frames the situation in a more positive light—as a situation that requires a response and perhaps one that you can better prepare for in the future.

Stress can help you.

Stress can help you reach out to others. Reaching out to others can be critical in addressing the threat causing your stress and is also critical to a meaningful life. Stress can also encourage you to care for others, and when you reach out to others, they can care for you. Realizing such compassion can be comforting. Undergoing stress and experiencing others' care can help you build resources for dealing with future adverse events. Stress can help build your resilience. The next time you face a similar situation (to one that initially caused stress), it may cause less stress because you will likely appraise it as less threatening, knowing you have the resources to deal with it.

Try to generate positive emotions in stressful situations.

This rule can be tricky to enact, but positive emotions increase your attentional awareness and cognitive capacity for creativity, which may help you deal with stressful situations.

Use stress to push yourself.

When you appraise a situation as critical and challenging, stress represents a trigger to exerting effort in the current situation. You can use stress to push yourself mentally, but be careful and watch for physical strain. Some stress is good, but too much can take a physical toll.

6 Simple Rule: Build Your Entrepreneurial Team's Emotional Intelligence to Enhance Its Performance

Enhance your interpersonal understanding of those in your team.

Suppose you have a deeper understanding of the people with whom you interact. In that case, you can develop your knowledge of their emotional experiences and how to help regulate those emotional experiences and associated responses. This interpersonal knowledge may not necessarily come only from experiences in the work context. Perhaps this is why team-building exercises can be effective outside of the work context.

Reflect on your team's processes and outcomes.

It would be best if you reflected on your team's processes and outcomes to improve those processes for enhanced entrepreneurial performance. Reflecting on the emotional inputs and outcomes throughout the entrepreneurial process can help build team-level emotional intelligence. These reflections can be performed at the team level, but that requires a psychologically safe climate within your team. People need to feel comfortable talking about their own and others' emotions. It would be best to create a psychologically safe environment so that your team members can reflect on the emotional aspects of their processes and outcomes.

Seek outside feedback about your team's emotional intelligence.

While it is essential for your team to reflect and provide feedback to team members, it is also essential to receive feedback from those outside your team. This outside perspective of your team's emotional intelligence can help provide critical feedback as an essential source of improvement and learning.

Confront team members' errant behavior.

Being an emotionally intelligent team does not mean that the team is soft. Indeed, it is the opposite: if a team member deviates from team norms, your team must have some mechanism for communicating this source of dysfunction. It might be as simple as saying, "Did you get out of bed on the wrong side this morning?" or "Why are you so grumpy today?" The focal team member may have a reason for their negative emotions. Discussing that reason may allow you to help the individual with the underlying problem and their negative emotional experience.

This ability at an emotional level represents team-level emotional intelligence.

Care for each other.

An entrepreneurial team is more effective when it cooperates and coordinates. Cooperation and coordination are enhanced when team members care for each other and the team as a whole. This caring can manifest as compassion when a team member suffers from an external event or the team suffers from an organizationally adverse event. Emotionally intelligent teams are self-compassionate and demonstrate compassion to other teams within and outside the venture.

Establish norms for emotion regulation.

Emotional intelligence can represent a capability of a venture or an entrepreneurial team if the detection, evaluation, and regulation of emotions are established through some norms, processes, or routines. For example, you may want to provide your team with an outlet for negative emotions, such as a punching bag in the corner of the office.

11

Simples Rules for Developing the Social Aspects of Your Venture

1 Simple Rule: Do Amazing Things with Your Venture to Help Those Suffering

Invest (rather than conserve) personal resources to help those suffering.

Adverse events (such as natural or artificial disasters) may cause you to lose some of your physical resources and suffer. Investing your resources to help other suffering people can improve their lives and your functioning.

These research articles provided important information in formulating the following simple rules for developing the social aspects of your venture: (1) Farny, S., Kibler, E., Hai, S., & Landoni, P. (2019). Volunteer retention in prosocial venturing: The role of emotional connectivity. *Entrepreneurship Theory and Practice, 43*(6), 1094–1123. . (2) Grimes, M. G., Williams, T. A., & Zhao, E. (2019). Anchors aweigh: The sources, variety, and challenges of mission drift. *Academy of Management Review, 44*(4), 819–845. (3) Mittermaier, A., Patzelt, H., & Shepherd, D. A. (2023). Motivating prosocial venturing in response to a humanitarian crisis: Building theory from the refugee crisis in Germany. *Entrepreneurship Theory and Practice, 47*(3), 924–963. (4) Mittermaier, A., Shepherd, D. A., & Patzelt, H.

D. A. Shepherd et al., *66 Simple Rules for Entrepreneurs*,
https://doi.org/10.1007/978-3-031-62032-4_11

Offer compassion to those who are suffering.
Take entrepreneurial action to respond to the uncertainty of a crisis and help others. Your entrepreneurial action can help overcome constraints to deliver compassionate products and services that are customized and delivered urgently at a large scale and scope.

Invest personal resources to build personal resources.
Investing your resources to help those suffering can make you more resilient. By engaging in compassion venturing (entrepreneurial action to alleviate the suffering of others), you can meet other positive people who can make a positive difference. These interactions can have a positive impact on you. Your help may also cause people to express gratitude. That gratitude can help you generate positive emotions, which also represent a resource. For example, helping others can strengthen relationships. Relationships are critical to resilience. Moreover, taking action and making a positive difference can increase your coping self-efficacy. Coping self-efficacy is believing you can successfully deal with adverse events. This coping self-efficacy provides positive beliefs that enable you to cope successfully with subsequent adverse events.

You likely have more resources than you imagine.
Even though adverse events can take away many physical resources, people are often left with intangible resources. By investing in those intangible resources, you can help alleviate suffering. These intangible resources include local knowledge, customs, and relationships. Use them to make a positive difference in people's lives.

(2022). We cannot direct the wind, but we can adjust the sails: Prosocial ventures' responses to potential resource threats. *Organization Science, 33*(3), 1116–1141. (5) Patzelt, H., & Shepherd, D. A. (2024). A fatigue model of social venturing. *Small Business Economics*, advance online publication. (6) Williams, T. A., & Shepherd, D. A. (2016). Victim entrepreneurs doing well by doing good: Venture creation and well-being in the aftermath of a resource shock. *Journal of Business Venturing, 31*(4), 365–387. (7) Williams, T. A., & Shepherd, D. A. (2018). To the rescue!? Brokering a rapid, scaled and customized compassionate response to suffering after disaster. *Journal of Management Studies, 55*(6), 910–942. (8) Williams, T. A., & Shepherd, D. A. (2021). Bounding and binding: Trajectories of community-organization emergence following a major disruption. *Organization Science, 32*(3), 824–855.

Use bricolage to make the most of remaining resources.

Bricolage involves using the resources you have at hand, combining them, and recombining them to use them in ways they were not originally conceived. This creative behavior can generate essential solutions that help alleviate others' suffering.

2 Simple Rule: Align Your Motivation with the Type of Venture You Want to Build

Know why you want to help those suffering.

While some entrepreneurs found ventures to alleviate suffering primarily based on the compassion they feel for those in need, others use such ventures also to fulfill their personal goals, such as being independent or learning. If you know your motivations, you can build the venture that fits you best. If you are mainly driven by compassion, your venture should provide quick and scalable help by acquiring a large base of resource providers. If you see your venture as a means for becoming independent and developing yourself, try to develop a sustainable business model by evaluating multiple opportunities for help and building a solid team around you.

Focus on the right activities to maximize your impact.

Depending on the type of venture you are building, you may focus on different activities to meet your goals. If you want to help many people in need and do so quickly, you should focus on execution. In this case, you should concentrate on setting up a clear structure for your venture that allows you to distribute tasks and resources efficiently. If you aim for a more long-term solution, your structure should be flexible to adjust to feedback and the changing needs of those you help and your stakeholders.

Develop and balance dual logics.

Suppose you want to build a venture that helps others. In that case, you need to pursue multiple goals—financial goals to keep your venture running, social goals to help others, and/or perhaps even ecological goals if you want to address environmental problems. These different logics need to be built into your venture's mission. Balancing/emphasizing different logics is not easy but requires thorough consideration because your venture's mission can impact which stakeholders and resource providers you can attract to your venture and your ability to find opportunities.

Be aware of mission drift.
One of the challenges you face when pursuing multiple logics is that your mission can drift toward one goal over time while neglecting the other(s). Although there might be good reasons for this, mission drift can decrease stakeholder commitment and damage your reputation. If you realize your venture's mission is drifting, explain to stakeholders why this is the case and emphasize your venture's positive impact.

Be open to criticism and take responsibility for your mission (drift).

Even if you have the best intentions and have helped many people, some may criticize aspects of your venture as not being social or sustainable enough. Rather than justifying this critique by referring to the many good things you have achieved, try to embrace it. By critically thinking about how you can improve, you can build an even stronger venture with more impact.

3 Simple Rule: Be Sensitive to the Needs of Your Venture Members

Attract people with strong prosocial motivation.
To maximize your venture's impact, you may consider attracting helpers based on their qualifications to fulfill the tasks at hand. However, given that a strong social mission often does not allow you to pay employees high salaries, make sure that they share the social motivation of your

venture; otherwise, they may quickly leave once they receive offers with higher salaries and better promotion opportunities.

Invest time to keep your venture members motivated.

While motivating employees is critical for any venture, it is particularly challenging for ventures with a social mission because they only have limited resources for financial compensation. Therefore, you must invest time and effort to create an atmosphere that employees, particularly volunteers, enjoy. You may have to invest considerable time in communication, conflict management, trust-building, and a strong organizational identity and culture. In doing so, you ensure that all "pull the cart" in the right direction.

Make employees and volunteers emotionally connected to your venture.
The dual logics pursued by your venture mission can create ambivalence and rejection of some venture activities by members. To understand these members' feelings, you can put yourself in their shoes by establishing meetings and platforms where they can share conflict experiences and discuss the feelings caused by your venture's dual mission. To counteract aversive feelings, energize your employees and volunteers. Try to induce excitement and enthusiasm for your venture by crafting a vision about the future outcomes of the venture's activities or by establishing rituals that enhance engagement with the venture.

Actively address declining volunteer commitment.
Sometimes, unforeseen external developments, such as economic crises or misconduct by some of the individuals you are trying to help, can diminish the motivation of volunteers. Closely monitor your environment for such potential threats. If you recognize potentially threatening events and circumstances, counteract decreasing volunteer commitment proactively. Try to emphasize the positive aspects of what you have achieved so far and remind volunteers that those in need may suffer most from a crisis and need even more help and that most of them are not accountable for the misconduct of a few. You may also want to reinforce your venture's identity and culture by establishing more

frequent meetings and generally enhancing communication with venture members.

4 Simple Rule: Don't Burnout in Pursuing Your Venture's Social Mission

Manage your compassion.

Your compassion for those suffering has motivated you to make social goals part of your venture's mission. However, there is always more suffering than one entrepreneur or venture can address. As for many engaged in social work, your compassion may drive you to invest more personal and psychological resources than you have, leading to fatigue and burnout. Carefully monitor your energy levels and take regular breaks to recharge emotionally.

Monitor your passion for helping those in need.

You can avoid fatigue by pursuing a social mission with your venture. An essential element of avoiding fatigue is being passionate about what you do. If your passion is high, you will feel energized, rather than exhausted, from helping others. When you feel your passion declining, take a break to fill up your battery and regain passion for what you are doing.

Be self-compassionate.

While we often feel compassion for others, we tend to be harder on ourselves. The more you care about yourself and acknowledge that everyone makes mistakes, the more you will have the energy to help others.

Build support networks.

Although some entrepreneurs see themselves as the lonely hero at the helm of a venture, particularly if they pursue a social mission, this view can be dangerous. Support from family, friends, mentors, and other entrepreneurs can be crucial for coping with social venturing demands.

Support networks can provide important resources and emotional encouragement and can make you more resilient to the high demands of helping others. You can build these networks as part of your venturing activities, at networking events, or within incubation programs. Try to frequently interact and communicate with others within and outside your venture.

Be prepared to cope with negative feedback.
Since you are helping others, you might expect gratitude rather than complaints from those being helped. While negative feedback might be hard to swallow and may drain your energy at first, consider it as a source for improvement. Perhaps you can enhance your venture's helping activities so that more people are served, or maybe your help offers can be improved by listening more to victims about what they need.

12

Simple Rules for Managing Mistakes and Failures

1 Simple Rule: To Be Successful, You Need to Be Prepared for and Manage Failure

Reflect on the relationship between uncertainty, opportunities, and failure.

Opportunities are identified in uncertain environments. Making decisions under uncertainty can mean you are sometimes wrong, potentially leading to failure. Therefore, failure is a common outcome in the pursuit of opportunities. Rather than thinking of failure as something that isolates you from others, you need to recognize that it is a common

---

These research articles provided important information in formulating the following simple rules for managing your mistakes and failures: (1) McMullen, J. S., Shepherd, D. A., & Patzelt, H. (2009). Managerial (in) attention to competitive threats. *Journal of Management Studies, 46*(2), 157–181. (2) Schweitzer, M. E., Brooks, A. W., & Galinsky, A. D. (2015). The organizational apology. *Harvard Business Review, 94*(9), 44–52. (3) Shepherd, D. A. (2003). Learning from business failure: Propositions of grief recovery for the self-employed. *Academy of Management Review, 28*(2), 318–328. (4) Shepherd, D. A., Patzelt, H., & Wolfe, M. (2011). Moving forward from project failure: Negative emotions, affective commitment, and learning from experience. *Academy of Management Journal, 54*(6), 1229–1259.

D. A. Shepherd et al., *66 Simple Rules for Entrepreneurs*,
https://doi.org/10.1007/978-3-031-62032-4_12

outcome experienced by many entrepreneurs. You want to use failure to learn but also keep the cost low.

Consider succeeding by increasing your attempts.

This statement means that to achieve success, you have to keep trying. To hit more home runs, you need to have more at-bats. The hope is that with more tries, you learn to convert more of them to success. However, failure is still an intimate part of the entrepreneurial process. It is essential that you can cope with and learn from your entrepreneurial failures.

Use failure to create a sense of urgency.

Failure does not feel good. It means that something important has been lost, which creates a sense of urgency to learn from the process. Use that sense of urgency; don't suppress it. After learning from the process, hopefully, you will feel more capable of taking subsequent entrepreneurial action.

Analyze and learn from near misses.

A common reaction to a near miss is to consider yourself lucky and move on. The attributes of a near miss are similar to those of a failure; however, a near miss does not have the emotional baggage of a failure. Therefore, while we rarely use near misses to learn, we should. However, without the urgency of a failure, we need to motivate ourselves to invest the effort to learn from these near misses. Don't waste these information-rich sources of learning.

Use real options reasoning to terminate ventures.

You can consider your venture as a portfolio of opportunities. Each opportunity is like an option in that it gives you the right to exploit the potential opportunity but not the obligation to do so. When one opportunity shows a lack of promise, you need to terminate that opportunity and redeploy resources to those that show more promise. While you may consider these terminations failures, they actually increase your chance of overall venture success, especially if you can complete them quickly and cheaply.

Use failure to build intuition.

You can learn more from your failures than your successes. Use failures to enhance your intuition. However, sometimes, we want to focus on our successes and ignore our failures. This approach can mean that our intuition has a survivor bias, which might be dangerous to rely on. Informed intuition can be very useful for you in the entrepreneurial context. Make sure you use both successes and failures to develop your intuition.

2 Simple Rule: Yes, You Can Learn More from Your Failures than Your Successes, but It Can Be More Challenging than You Think

Be aware that you may have attribution and antifailure biases.

It is natural to have an antifailure bias. None of us like failure. We often attribute successes to our skills and knowledge to protect our egos and failures to external causes. These attributes can lead to superstitious learning. It would be best to overcome this natural tendency because it obstructs learning. If a failure is attributed to external causes, then there is nothing for you to learn. You are helpless. Instead, asking yourself what you could have done differently to avoid the failure is better. This question puts you in the mindset to learn something from your failure experiences.

Realize that it is natural to feel grief when a project is terminated.

Grief is a negative emotional reaction to the loss of something important. If you feel grief when an opportunity is terminated or a project fails, it simply means it was important to you. Most people feel grief when they lose something important. While this grief can highlight the importance of a failure, it can represent an emotional obstacle to learning from the experience. Learning from a failure is easier if you are able to overcome this emotional obstacle. Therefore, learning from failures is rarely automatic or instantaneous. Overcoming this emotional obstacle involves a process of dealing with grief—not necessarily eliminating grief but holding it in balance so that it does not overwhelm your thinking.

Do not seek to normalize or become desensitized to failure.

One way to reduce the emotional obstacle to learning from your failures is to normalize failure or become desensitized to it. However, the problem with taking emotions out of entrepreneurial outcomes is that doing so likely eliminates emotions as an input to the entrepreneurial process. With less emotional input (e.g., passion), the entrepreneurial process is more likely to generate a failure. That failure is less likely to create the urgency to learn from the experience. Learning to regulate the negative emotions generated by failures is better than eliminating all negative emotional reactions.

Oscillate between a loss and a restoration orientation to regulate grief.

You can deal with the grief of a failure by engaging in a loss orientation. With a loss orientation, you focus on the failure to try and understand what happened; understanding the failure can help you break the emotional bonds to the lost project or venture. However, after a while, engaging in a loss orientation can generate more negative emotions, such as ruminations. You can then switch to a restoration orientation. With a restoration orientation, you focus on addressing secondary causes of stress (not the failure directly but the problems generated by the failure) and ignoring the failure to avoid the associated negative emotions. However, ignoring the failure and the emotions surrounding it can only be successful for so long. Eventually, they surface and create problems. Thus, to fully deal with the grief of a failure, you should oscillate between a loss orientation and a restoration orientation until your grief subsides.

Select and use emotionally intelligent friends to help you deal with failure.

Emotionally intelligent friends can tell when you feel negative emotions and know how to help you regulate them. They can help you oscillate between a loss orientation and a restoration orientation. It is good to have emotionally intelligent friends. You can also develop an emotionally capable organization by establishing routines and processes for noticing and regulating the negative emotions of venture members, such as social support groups and routines for dealing with failures.

Develop and use self-compassion.

Self-compassion refers to helping yourself when you are suffering, such as experiencing grief over a failure. You can show yourself self-compassion by engaging in self-kindness. Be kind to yourself when you are suffering. Think about what you would say to a suffering friend and use the same approach with yourself. Show yourself self-compassion by realizing that everybody fails at some point. This recognition can help ensure you do not isolate yourself from others. Many others have also experienced what you are feeling. Show yourself self-compassion by engaging in emotional mindfulness—that is, acknowledge your negative emotions but hold them evenly without allowing them to overwhelm your decision-making.

3 Simple Rule: You Cannot Choose to Be Error Free; You Need to Choose Which Error You Will Regret Less

Calculate the costs of acting and being wrong (error of commission) versus right (a hit).

You may think that a signal represents an opportunity, but you could be wrong given the uncertainty surrounding that signal. Alternatively, your interpretation of the signal may be correct, and there is an opportunity worth pursuing. Consider the costs of acting relative to the benefits of acting.

Calculate the costs of not acting and being wrong (an error of omission) versus right (a correct rejection).

Given the uncertainty surrounding a signal, you may decide not to act on it based on your assessment that it represents noise. Alternatively, there may be a cost if the signal represents an opportunity you pass over. Consider the costs of inaction relative to the benefits of inaction.

Consider the payoff matrix when making your decisions.

By considering (1) acting and being right (a hit), (2) acting and being wrong (a false alarm), (3) not acting and being right (correct rejection), and (4) not acting and being wrong (a miss), you have developed a payoff matrix. It may be challenging to compare different aspects of these costs and benefits directly, but at least the payoff matrix highlights salient considerations for an important decision.

Reflect on which you will regret more.

People often ignore their payoff matrix by considering potential feelings of regret. They choose the type of error—either an error of commission or an error of omission—by choosing to act or not act based on which error has the lowest anticipated regret. As an entrepreneur, you may regret an error of omission. That is, you may regret not acting and missing out on an opportunity. Think about your payoff matrix and anticipate your possible regrets (i.e., an error of commission [a false alarm] versus an error of omission [a miss]).

Consider what is normal.

You may want to consider what is normal under the current situation. If it is normal to act, then if you act and you're mistaken, you will experience less regret than if you did not act and were wrong. For example, a firefighter is more likely to regret omission errors than commission errors. However, if it is normal not to act, you may regret an omission error more than a commission error. It is worth considering which errors you can live with and which you cannot.

4 Simple Rule: Prepare for Crises Because They Will Probably Happen (You Just Don't Know What or When)

Build your resilience in preparation for a crisis.

You are resilient when you can maintain positive functioning under adversity. However, you may be unable to anticipate the adverse events that will impact you and your venture. Still, you can build your own and your venture's resilience to better prepare for these unexpected events.

Build resilience by developing coping self-efficacy.

Coping self-efficacy is the belief that one can successfully engage in tasks to overcome the challenges of a threat. People who develop high coping self-efficacy from previous adverse experiences perform better in the face of other events that require coping. You can build your coping self-efficacy by reflecting on when you successfully navigated an adverse event. Coping with small adverse events can help build your coping self-efficacy for successfully dealing with more hostile adverse events.

Build resilience through optimism.

Optimism involves envisioning a positive future. With optimism, you will see adversity as a temporary situation—a situation that you can change. Believing that you can do something to improve your situation means that you will be proactive toward finding a solution and persist with that action. In contrast, a more pessimistic approach can lead to helplessness. Helplessness involves a feeling of lack of control over what happens to you and thus a belief that trying to change your situation is pointless. Be optimistic in the face of adversity because it can be a positive, self-fulfilling prophecy.

Invest rather than conserve resources in a crisis.

When a crisis or adverse event hits, you can either conserve your resources for use later or invest your resources now. Entrepreneurs who invest their resources in a crisis tend to do better than those who conserve. If you invest your resources, you are taking positive action to improve the lives of others. In doing so, you will see others doing the same, offering you gratitude and a unique opportunity to develop your competence. These outcomes of investing yourself in acting to help others all positively impact your resilience to this crisis or adverse event and subsequent adversities and crises.

Build resilience by creating and maintaining strong relationships. Strong relationships provide critical resources in the face of an adverse event. They are based on trust and offer emotional and psychological support. The challenging conditions of an adverse event that drive you to rely on these relationships provide the opportunity to strengthen these relationships further. Therefore, using these relationships represents resilience and also builds resilience resources.

Reflect on your trial-by-fire experiences.

Trial by fire is when you have faced adversity and come out through the other side. You survived and developed some habits and mental strategies that can now be used in a more favorable (postadversity) environment. This trial by fire has enabled you to build highly effective capabilities. Realizing that the hardships you have faced in the past represent trial by fire provides you confidence that you now have the capabilities to cope with current adversity and achieve success.

5 Simple Rule: If You Caused a Mistake that Was a Core Violation of Your Entrepreneurial Venture and Negatively Impacts Others, Then You Better Make a Good Apology

Be candid about the cause.

Be honest about the cause of the mistake. Don't compound the mistake with an unbelievable cause for it or find out later that your stated cause was incorrect. Without a candid response to the cause of the failure, the rest of the attributes of a good apology will have no effect.

Feel and show remorse for your mistakes.

The mistake has harmed other people, and you need to show the appropriate negative emotions given that harm. These negative emotions indicate that you understand the harm caused and are motivated to change.

Detail your commitment to change.

Explain to those impacted by your mistake that you understand it, the harm it has created, and how your actions caused it. Use that understanding to indicate how you will change in the future.

Change.

You must act on your knowledge and admissions of the cause of the mistake, your remorse for the mistake, and your commitment to change by actually changing. People accept others making mistakes if they show that they have learned from the mistakes and tried to make amends.

13

Simple Rules for Exiting Your Entrepreneurial Venture

1 Simple Rule: If You Want to End Your Entrepreneurial Journey, Consider Multiple Possibilities

Consider potential exit routes early in your venture's life.

Every entrepreneur has to exit their venture one day (unless you want to "die in the saddle"). However, not every venture fits every exit route. If you try to take your company public one day, you must set up a venture that can grow enough to be eligible for stock market listings. If you want

---

These research articles provided important information in formulating the following simple rules for exiting your entrepreneurial venture: (1) DeTienne, D. R., & Cardon, M. S. (2012). Impact of founder experience on exit intentions. *Small Business Economics, 38*(4), 351– 374. (2) Kandade, K., Samara, G., Parada, M. J., & Dawson, A. (2021). From family successors to successful business leaders: A qualitative study of how high-quality relationships develop in family businesses. *Journal of Family Business Strategy, 12*(2), 100334. (3) LeCounte, J. F. (2022). Founder-CEOs: Succession planning for the success, growth, and legacy of family firms. *Journal of Small Business Management, 60*(3), 616– 633. (4) Lee, J. M., Yoon, D., & Boivie, S. (2020). Founder CEO succession: The role of CEO organizational identification. *Academy of Management Journal, 63*(1), 224– 245. (5) Wennberg, K., Wiklund, J., DeTienne, D. R., & Cardon, M. S. (2010). Reconceptualizing entrepreneurial exit: Divergent exit routes and their drivers. *Journal of Business Venturing, 25*(4), 361–375.

D. A. Shepherd et al., *66 Simple Rules for Entrepreneurs*,
https://doi.org/10.1007/978-3-031-62032-4_13

to keep the venture alive after exit to offer your employees a future in the firm, develop a strategic fit for a potential buyer. If you want to leave the firm to your offspring, employ them beforehand to familiarize them with the firm and gain employee support. Thus, your options for exiting the venture are influenced by the decisions you make earlier in the venture's life.

Don't underestimate the emotional costs of an exit.

Although your exit may be voluntary, substantial emotions are likely associated with leaving the firm. Some entrepreneurs compare this process with a kid leaving the house. After the exit, you may feel that something important is missing in your life. Anticipate these emotions to be better able to "let go." Your partner or loved ones can be an essential source of support in this process. Try to consider how you want to spend your time after the exit. Engage in outside activities before the exit for inspiration.

Plan your venture exit and your exit flexibly.

Planning your exit is difficult and can be time-consuming. In addition, some factors influencing your exit options, such as economic developments, are out of your control. Therefore, plan your exit some time ahead and account for potential contingencies. Consider the possibility that a potential buyer for your venture may require you to continue working for the venture for some time to share your knowledge. Conversely, if you believe your venture has great economic potential, you may retain a stake even after ceasing your operational involvement.

Consider starting again.

After exiting their ventures, many entrepreneurs want to feel the excitement of starting up again. Given all your experiences from the exit, you are uniquely positioned to "do it again." Not only have you acquired essential knowledge, but you may also have unique networks and financial means for making a new startup successful.

2 Simple Rule: To Keep Your Venture Alive After Exit, Manage the Succession Process Right

Select the proper successor.

You may find potential successors for you inside or outside the firm. Don't look for a copy of yourself; you are unlikely to find one. Instead, look for someone with the right skills based on their resume and who is highly motivated to make the firm successful. Internal candidates have the advantage of knowing your firm, but external candidates bring new ideas that may take the firm to the next level. Decide on the right candidate based on your venture's current and future perspectives.

Plan the succession process strategically.

Founder succession is not a one-time event but a complex process that can take years. Plan the process. The more you involve your successor early in succession planning, the more likely they will accept the plan and work jointly with you on its execution for a smooth transition.

Develop your successor.

Your successor needs time to learn from you and understand your business's operations, culture, and identity and your role as a leader. Help your successor take over this role. This help can include developing your successor's technical and business skills and providing mentoring and emotional support. Recognize the successor's education and achievements. Trust in their abilities and let them make mistakes. Mentor them and provide them unconditional support without expecting returns.

Use advisors to manage the emotions of the succession process.

The succession process is emotional and stressful for both you, the exiting entrepreneur, and your successor. Advisors can help unearth and alleviate these emotions. They can also mitigate conflict that generates undesired emotions. By understanding your successor's emotions, you can better assist them in taking over your role. This understanding will make the succession process smoother and more successful.

Let the successor do their job.

Since nobody knows a venture as well as the founder, you may think you are indispensable to your firm. However, interfering with your successor makes it difficult for them to realize their ideas and gain other venture members' respect. Be approachable for the successor's requests for advice, but avoid their decision-making and management. Otherwise, you jeopardize the firm's success perspective—the opposite of what you tried to achieve when selecting and installing the successor in the first place.

14

Conclusion

In our jobs as business professors, we have seen many entrepreneurs start new ventures. Some of these entrepreneurs failed, others thrived, and a few of them were more successful than they (and we) had ever imagined. We studied them over many years, trying to understand what explains their successes and failures. As academics, we dove deeply into their problems and challenges. Many answers we gained from our studies were complex and difficult to explain to others, including the entrepreneurs we studied.

In this book, we focused on easy-to-understand answers. We distilled them from our many studies and infused them with insights from our colleagues' work. The result is 66 simple rules, each including several subrules. These simple rules cover the entire entrepreneurial journey.

We started by explaining simple rules for recognizing new business opportunities. These rules emphasize the premise of starting the entrepreneurial journey and illustrate how you should consider finding a creative idea as the basis for your potential venture.

In the subsequent chapter, we presented simple rules for selecting markets and making decisions related to market entry. These rules introduce you to approaches that will help you gather and act on information

D. A. Shepherd et al., *66 Simple Rules for Entrepreneurs*,
https://doi.org/10.1007/978-3-031-62032-4_14

that you need for these decisions. They also illustrate how to advance your venture if your first business model fails.

You must make many important decisions at different steps of the entrepreneurial journey. Therefore, we presented simple rules that entail easy principles and tools for making decisions under typical entrepreneurial circumstances—namely, high uncertainty and resource scarcity. An essential part of these rules also illustrates that you—like everybody—may be fooled by decision-making biases, so we also provided advice for what you can do to minimize these biases.

We also offered simple rules to help you develop plans and strategies to advance your venture. These rules demonstrate how you can convert your personal goals and preferences into a plan for your venture. They also tell you how to make your venture more robust and resilient in the face of obstacles.

The following chapter considered that entrepreneurship occurs in a social context and thus provided simple rules for managing stakeholders. These rules address how you can engage with others to develop your opportunity and venture. We focused on who you should engage with and how you should interact and communicate to ensure you can access the knowledge and resources you need for building your venture.

The next chapter then focused on one particular group of people that is key for venture development: the entrepreneurial team. In another set of simple rules, we introduced you to building a strong team and how to interact with your cofounders to make the most out of your team's competencies.

Further, we presented simple rules for managing your employees. We discussed who you might attract to your venture and how you can lead them to build a strong culture as a critical asset for your venture.

For many entrepreneurs, growing their ventures is an important goal. Therefore, the subsequent chapter introduced several simple rules that will help you maximize your venture's growth potential. In particular, the rules will help you prepare for the growth journey. Again, the rules emphasize the importance of culture for venture development and growth.

During the entrepreneurial journey, all founders experience emotional ups and downs. Thus, the subsequent chapter presented simple rules that will help you manage and channel your emotions. These rules also offer some advice for coping with the high stress levels you will likely experience during challenging times.

Not all entrepreneurs are alike, and some emphasize developing the social aspects of their ventures. Therefore, we presented simple rules that illustrate the many good things you can do for others with your venture. These rules also acknowledge, however, that engaging in a social mission can drain your energy and lead to fatigue. We thus offered advice on how to avoid fatigue from social venturing.

Given the high uncertainty of the entrepreneurial journey, all entrepreneurs make mistakes and experience errors and failures. Accordingly, we offered some simple rules that can help you learn from these mistakes and failures, which is neither automatic nor easy.

Finally, one day, every entrepreneurial journey comes to an end. Therefore, we concluded this book with simple rules for exiting your venture and ensuring succession goes smoothly.

Driving Route 66 is an adventure. Going on the entrepreneurial journey is an adventure. Just as simple traffic rules help you navigate perhaps the most famous road in the world, we hope the simple rules offered in this book prevent you from getting lost along your entrepreneurial journey but instead reach the successful outcome you want to achieve.

References and Additional Readings

Amabile, T. M. (1997). Motivating creativity in organizations: On doing what you love and loving what you do. *California Management Review, 40*(1), 39–58.

Amabile, T., Fisher, C. M., & Pillemer, J. (2014). IDEO's culture of helping. *Harvard Business Review, 92*(1), 54–61.

Bhide, A. (1996). The questions every entrepreneur must answer. *Harvard Business Review, 74*(6), 120.

Bohn, R. (2000). Stop fighting fires. *Harvard Business Review, 78*, 82–92.

Breugst, N. (2023). *Entrepreneurial teams*. Oxford University Press.

Breugst, N., & Shepherd, D. A. (2017). If you fight with me, I'll get mad! A social model of entrepreneurial affect. *Entrepreneurship Theory and Practice, 41*(3), 379–418.

Breugst, N., Domurath, A., Patzelt, H., & Klaukien, A. (2012). Perceptions of entrepreneurial passion and employees' commitment to entrepreneurial ventures. *Entrepreneurship: Theory & Practice, 36*(1), 171–192.

Breugst, N., Patzelt, H., & Rathgeber, P. (2015). How should we divide the pie? Equity distribution and its impact on entrepreneurial teams. *Journal of Business Venturing, 30*(1), 66–94.

Breugst, N., Patzelt, H., & Shepherd, D. A. (2020). When is effort contagious in new venture management teams? Understanding the contingencies of social motivation theory. *Journal of Management Studies, 57*(8), 1556–1588.

D. A. Shepherd et al., *66 Simple Rules for Entrepreneurs*,
https://doi.org/10.1007/978-3-031-62032-4

Breugst, N., Preller, R., Patzelt, H., & Shepherd, D. A. (2018). Information reliability and team reflection as contingencies of the relationship between information elaboration and team decision quality. *Journal of Organizational Behavior, 39*(10), 1314–1329.

Brinckmann, J., Grichnik, D., & Kapsa, D. (2010). Should entrepreneurs plan or just storm the castle? A meta-analysis on contextual factors impacting the business planning–performance relationship in small firms. *Journal of Business Venturing, 25*(1), 24–40.

Brown, C. (2015). *Know your worth, and then ask for it.* TEDxColumbusWomen. https://www.ted.com/talks/casey_brown_know_your_worth_and_then_ask_for_it?language=en

Brown, T. (2008). Design thinking. *Harvard Business Review, 86*(6), 84–92.

Cacciotti, G., Hayton, J. C., Mitchell, J. R., & Giazitzoglu, A. (2016). A reconceptualization of fear of failure in entrepreneurship. *Journal of Business Venturing, 31*(3), 302–325.

Choi, Y., & Shepherd, D. (2004). Entrepreneurs' decisions to exploit opportunities. *Journal of Management, 30*(3), 377–395.

DeTienne, D. R., & Cardon, M. S. (2012). Impact of founder experience on exit intentions. *Small Business Economics, 38*(4), 351–374.

Domurath, A., Taggar, S., & Patzelt, H. (2023). A contingency model of employees' turnover intent in young ventures. *Small Business Economics,* forthcoming.

Druskat, V. U., & Wolff, S. B. (2001). Building the emotional intelligence of groups. *Harvard Business Review, 79*(3), 80–91.

Dyer, J. H., Gregersen, H. B., & Christensen, C. M. (2009). The innovator's DNA. *Harvard Business Review, 87*(12), 60–67.

Earley, P. C., & Mosakowski, E. (2004). Cultural intelligence. *Harvard Business Review, 82*(10), 139–146.

Eisenhardt, K. M. (1990). Speed and strategic choice: How managers accelerate decision making. *California Management Review, 32*(3), 39–54.

Eisenhardt, K. M., & Sull, D. N. (2001). Strategy as simple rules. *Harvard Business Review, 79*(1), 106–119.

El-Awad, Z., Brattström, A., & Breugst, N. (2022). Bridging cognitive scripts in multidisciplinary academic spinoff teams: A process perspective on how academics learn to work with non-academic managers. *Research Policy, 51*(10), 104592.

Farny, S., Kibler, E., Hai, S., & Landoni, P. (2019). Volunteer retention in prosocial venturing: The role of emotional connectivity. *Entrepreneurship Theory and Practice, 43*(6), 1094–1123.

Farson, R., & Keyes, R. (2006). The failure-tolerant leader. *Managing Innovation and Change*, 249.

Fauchart, E., & Gruber, M. (2011). Darwinians, communitarians, and missionaries: The role of founder identity in entrepreneurship. *Academy of Management Journal, 54*(5), 935–957.

Gaglio, C. M., & Katz, J. A. (2001). The psychological basis of opportunity identification: Entrepreneurial alertness. *Small Business Economics, 16*(2), 95–111.

Garvin, D. A., & Roberto, M. A. (2001). What you don't know about making decisions. *Harvard Business Review, 79*(8), 108–119.

Garvin, D. A., Edmondson, A. C., & Gino, F. (2008). Is yours a learning organization? *Harvard Business Review, 86*(3), 109–116.

Gasper, K., & Clore, G. L. (2002). Attending to the big picture: Mood and global versus local processing of visual information. *Psychological Science, 13*(1), 34–40.

Goleman, D., & Boyatzis, R. (2017). Emotional intelligence has 12 elements. Which do you need to work on. *Harvard Business Review, 84*(2), 1–5.

Greiner, L. E. (1972). Evolution and revolution as organisations grow. *Harvard Business Review, 50*(4), 37–46.

Grimes, M. G., Williams, T. A., & Zhao, E. (2019). Anchors aweigh: The sources, variety, and challenges of mission drift. *Academy of Management Review, 44*(4), 819–845.

Gruber, M., MacMillan, I. C., & Thompson, J. D. (2008). Look before you leap: Market opportunity identification in emerging technology firms. *Management Science, 54*(9), 1652–1665.

Kammerlander, N., & Breugst, N. (2019). Construals matter: Painting the big picture or drawing the brushstrokes of the family firm. *Family Business Review, 32*(3), 222–232.

Kandade, K., Samara, G., Parada, M. J., & Dawson, A. (2021). From family successors to successful business leaders: A qualitative study of how high-quality relationships develop in family businesses. *Journal of Family Business Strategy, 12*(2), 100334.

Kanze, D., Huang, L., Conley, M. A., & Higgins, E. T. (2018). We ask men to win and women not to lose: Closing the gender gap in startup funding. *Academy of Management Journal, 61*(2), 586–614.

Keeney, R. L., & Raiffa, H. (2006). The hidden traps in decision making. *Harvard Business Review, 84*(1), 118.

Kirtley, J., & O'Mahony, S. (2023). What is a pivot? Explaining when and how entrepreneurial firms decide to make strategic change and pivot. *Strategic Management Journal, 44*(1), 197–230.

Klaukien, A., Shepherd, D. A., & Patzelt, H. (2013). Passion for work, non-work related excitement, and innovation managers' decision to exploit new product opportunities. *Journal of Product Innovation Management, 30*(3), 574–588.

Lazar, M., Miron-Spektor, E., Agarwal, R., Erez, M., Goldfarb, B., & Chen, G. (2020). Entrepreneurial team formation. *Academy of Management Annals, 14*(1), 29–59.

LeCounte, J. F. (2022). Founder-CEOs: Succession planning for the success, growth, and legacy of family firms. *Journal of Small Business Management, 60*(3), 616–633.

Lee, J. M., Yoon, D., & Boivie, S. (2020). Founder CEO succession: The role of CEO organizational identification. *Academy of Management Journal, 63*(1), 224–245.

Malhotra, D. (2014). 15 Rules for negotiating a job offer. *Harvard Business Review, 92*(4), 117–120.

McGrath, R. G., & Keil, T. (2007). The value captor's process: Getting the most out of your new business ventures. *Harvard Business Review, 85*(5), 128–136.

McMullen, J. S., Shepherd, D. A., & Patzelt, H. (2009). Managerial (in) attention to competitive threats. *Journal of Management Studies, 46*(2), 157–181.

Mittermaier, A., Patzelt, H., & Shepherd, D. A. (2023). Motivating prosocial venturing in response to a humanitarian crisis: Building theory from the refugee crisis in Germany. *Entrepreneurship Theory and Practice, 47*(3), 924–963.

Mittermaier, A., Shepherd, D. A., & Patzelt, H. (2022). We cannot direct the wind, but we can adjust the sails: Prosocial ventures' responses to potential resource threats. *Organization Science, 33*(3), 1116–1141.

Patzelt, H., & Shepherd, D. A. (2024). A fatigue model of social venturing. *Small Business Economics*, advance online publication.

Patzelt, H., Behrens, J., Wolfe, M. T., & Shepherd, D. A. (2020). Perceived project transition support and employees' assessments of entrepreneurial project performance. *Journal of Business Venturing, 35*(1), 1–25.

Patzelt, H., Gartzia, L., Wolfe, M., & Shepherd, D. A. (2021). Managing negative emotions from entrepreneurial project failure: When and how does supportive leadership help employees? *Journal of Business Venturing, 36*(5), 106128.

Patzelt, H., Preller, R., & Breugst, N. (2021). Understanding the life cycles of entrepreneurial teams and their ventures: An agenda for future research. *Entrepreneurship Theory and Practice, 45*(5), 1119–1153.

Pohlmann, T., & Thomas, N. (2015). Relearning the art of asking questions. *Harvard Business Review*. https://hbr.org/2015/03/relearning-the-art-of-asking-questions

Preller, R., Breugst, N., Patzelt, H., & Dibbern, R. (2023). Team resilience building in response to co-founder exits. *Journal of Business Venturing, 38*(6), 106328.

Preller, R., Patzelt, H., & Breugst, N. (2020). Entrepreneurial visions in founding teams: Conceptualization, emergence, and effects on opportunity development. *Journal of Business Venturing, 35*(2), 105914.

Roach, M., & Sauermann, H. (2015). Founder or joiner? The role of preferences and context in shaping different entrepreneurial interests. *Management Science, 61*(9), 2160–2184.

Sarasvathy, S. D. (2001). Causation and effectuation: Toward a theoretical shift from economic inevitability to entrepreneurial contingency. *Academy of Management Review, 26*(2), 243–263.

Sauermann, H. (2018). Fire in the belly? Employee motives and innovative performance in start-ups versus established firms. *Strategic Entrepreneurship Journal, 12*(4), 423–454.

Schweitzer, M. E., Brooks, A. W., & Galinsky, A. D. (2015). The organizational apology. *Harvard Business Review, 94*(9), 44–52.

Seyb, S. K., Shepherd, D. A., & Williams, T. A. (2019). Exoskeletons, entrepreneurs, and communities: A model of co-constructing a potential opportunity. *Journal of Business Venturing, 34*(6).

Shepherd, D. A. (2003). Learning from business failure: Propositions of grief recovery for the self-employed. *Academy of Management Review, 28*(2), 318–328.

Shepherd, D. A., & Gruber, M. (2021). The lean startup framework: Closing the academic–practitioner divide. *Entrepreneurship Theory and Practice, 45*(5), 967–998.

Shepherd, D. A., Breugst, N., & Patzelt, H. (2023). A founding-team model of creating a venture's culture. *Journal of Business Venturing, 38*(2), 106286.

Shepherd, D. A., McMullen, J. S., & Ocasio, W. (2017). Is that an opportunity? An attention model of top managers' opportunity beliefs for strategic action. *Strategic Management Journal, 38*(3), 626–644.

Shepherd, D. A., Parida, V., & Wincent, J. (2020). The surprising duality of jugaad: Low firm growth and high inclusive growth. *Journal of Management Studies, 57*(1), 87–128.

Shepherd, D. A., Patzelt, H., & Wolfe, M. (2011). Moving forward from project failure: Negative emotions, affective commitment, and learning from experience. *Academy of Management Journal, 54*(6), 1229–1259.

Shepherd, D., Sattari, R., & Patzelt, H. (2022). A social model of opportunity development: Building and engaging communities of inquiry. *Journal of Business Venturing, 37*, 106033.

Soll, J. B., Milkman, K. L., & Payne, J. W. (2015). Outsmart your own biases. *Harvard Business Review, 93*(5), 64–71.

Soyer, E., & Hogarth, R. M. (2015). Fooled by experience. *Harvard Business Review, 93*(5), 72–77.

Tacke, F., Knockaert, M., Patzelt, H., & Breugst, N. (2023). When do greedy entrepreneurs exhibit unethical pro-organizational behavior? The role of new venture team trust. *Journal of Management, 49*(3), 974–1004.

Tryba, A., Patzelt, H., & Breugst, N. (2023). Knowledge diversity and venture growth: The contingent effects of early planning and experimentation. *British Journal of Management, 34*(1), 343–362.

Uzzi, B., & Dunlap, S. (2005). How to build your network. *Harvard Business Review, 83*(12), 53–60.

Van Lancker, E., Knockaert, M., Collewaert, V., & Breugst, N. (2023). Preparing for scaling: A study on founder role evolution. *Journal of Business Venturing, 38*(4), 106315.

Warnick, B. J., Murnieks, C. Y., McMullen, J. S., & Brooks, W. T. (2018). Passion for entrepreneurship or passion for the product? A conjoint analysis of angel and VC decision-making. *Journal of Business Venturing, 33*(3), 315–332.

Wasserman, N. (2012). *Founder's dilemmas: Anticipating and avoiding the pitfalls that can sink a startup*. Princeton University Press.

Wasserman, N. (2017). The throne vs. the kingdom: Founder control and value creation in startups. *Strategic Management Journal, 38*(2), 255–277.

Watkins, M. D., & Bazerman, M. H. (2003). Predictable surprises: The disasters you should have seen coming. *Harvard Business Review, 81*(3), 72–85.

Wennberg, K., Wiklund, J., DeTienne, D. R., & Cardon, M. S. (2010). Reconceptualizing entrepreneurial exit: Divergent exit routes and their drivers. *Journal of Business Venturing, 25*(4), 361–375.

Wiklund, J., & Shepherd, D. A. (2005). Entrepreneurial orientation and small business performance: A configurational approach. *Journal of Business Venturing, 20*, 71–91.

Wiklund, J., Patzelt, H., & Dimov, D. (2016). Entrepreneurship and psychological disorders: How ADHD can be productively harnessed. *Journal of Business Venturing Insights, 6*, 14–20.

Wiklund, J., Patzelt, H., & Shepherd, D. A. (2009). Building an integrative model of small business growth. *Small Business Economics, 32*(4), 351–374.

Williams, T. A., & Shepherd, D. A. (2016). Victim entrepreneurs doing well by doing good: Venture creation and well-being in the aftermath of a resource shock. *Journal of Business Venturing, 31*(4), 365–387.

Williams, T. A., & Shepherd, D. A. (2018). To the rescue!? Brokering a rapid, scaled and customized compassionate response to suffering after disaster. *Journal of Management Studies, 55*(6), 910–942.

Williams, T. A., & Shepherd, D. A. (2021). Bounding and binding: Trajectories of community-organization emergence following a major disruption. *Organization Science, 32*(3), 824–855.

Index

D. A. Shepherd et al., *66 Simple Rules for Entrepreneurs*,
https://doi.org/10.1007/978-3-031-62032-4

SPRINGER NATURE

GPSR Compliance

The European Union's (EU) General Product Safety Regulation (GPSR) is a set of rules that requires consumer products to be safe and our obligations to ensure this.

If you have any concerns about our products, you can contact us on ProductSafety@springernature.com

In case Publisher is established outside the EU, the EU authorized representative is:

Springer Nature Customer Service Center GmbH
Europaplatz 3
69115 Heidelberg, Germany

The manufacturer's authorised representative in the EU is Springer Nature Customer Service Centre GmbH, Europaplatz 3, 69115 Heidelberg, Germany. If you have any concerns regarding our products, please contact ProductSafety@springernature.com

Printed and bound by CPI Group (UK) Ltd, Croydon, CR0 4YY
01/10/2026
02225879-0006